HEARTS AND MINDS

"A RESOURCE BOOK OF LEARNING ACTIVITIES TO

AFFIRM DIVERSITY AND PROMOTE EQUALITY"

COPYRIGHT

ISBN-13: 978-1499131758

ISBN-10: 1499131755

ABOUT THE EDITOR

D. Constantine-Simms is an Occupational Psychologist, Counselling Psychologist and a qualified Therapeutic Career Coach. He is also as freelance print and photojournalist, whose work is regularly submitted and distributed by photo agencies such as Corbis Images and Demotix. His articles and images have appeared in British and international publications such as the Word (Canada) The Big Issue, The Guardian, The Voice Newspaper, Miami Times, and many other publications. Constantine-Simms has previously edited the following books and Co-edited Teachers for the Future (1995) The Greatest Taboo: Homosexuality in Black Communities (2001) Hip Hop Had a Dream: Vol. 1 the Artful Movement (2008) Constantine-Simms is the recipient of the 2001 Lambda Award for Best Anthology for his book: The Greatest Taboo: Homosexuality in Black Communities (2001).

CONTENTS

INTRODUCTION

Hearts and Minds is an excellent resource manual that's been designed to encourage participants by way of interactive exercises, mini-case studies and role play to achieve the following learning objectives.

1) Identify different types of discrimination

2) Examine their own cultural backgrounds

3) Raise awareness about prejudices and preconceptions

4) Empower a sense of human dignity and social responsibility

5) Recognize how cultural differences may impact behaviour.

6) Reduce conflict.

7) Acknowledge Stereotypes

8) Identify individual and organizational attitudes towards diversity and equality.

In order to achieve these objectives this resource book has been divided into the following eight sections.

1) Prejudice and Discrimination

2) The Role of Media Section

3) Lookism

4) Language and Diversity

5) Diversity and Equality

6) Power Privilege And Status

7) Stereotype Thinking

8) Cultural Diversity

Each activity is generally presented in the following format with variations:

1) Name, to identify the exercise

2) Brief description of the purpose of the exercise

3) Normal time allotment

4) Equipment required

5) Consumable materials needed

6) Procedures suggesting how the exercise should be conducted

7) Short conclusion section

8) Helpful trainers notes

Despite legislation compelling organizations to comply with anti-discrimination legislation and policies, the degree of compliance varies and in many respect can influence the impact and effectiveness of diversity and equality intervention strategies if the consultant does not familiarise themselves the following concepts below:

1. **The negative organization**: will not have an EOP or comply with the law. It will not claim to be an EOP employer. It may practice discrimination.

2. **The minimalist/partial organization:** This organization will declare itself to have an EOPE but in practice equality will have a low profile. It will not have developed procedures to over come discrimination. Most likely to adopt reactive approach and defend claims of discrimination.

3. **The compliant organization**: Will ensure that it fulfils its legal obligations through a formal policy approach. Also because anti-discrimination only covers three areas of law, sex, race, disability, this organization will have a very narrow agenda.

4. **The comprehensive proactive organization:** Will ensure it complies with the law, but will be concerned to monitor the outcomes of policy and practice in order to assess their impact. Positive action initiatives will be a feature of policy here to ensure that the agenda moves beyond tackling discrimination toward promoting equality.

The degree of organizational compliance varies and as previously stated, consultants should design and deliver their training to address the culture of the organization in relation to the following traits:

1. **Monolithic organizations;** which have a large majority of one demographic group (typically white males), especially in higher level positions. Women and minority group employees are expected to adopt the norms and values of the majority group in order to survive.

2. **Pluralistic organizations;** are more mixed in composition than monolithic organizations, primarily because they take more steps to hire and promote minority group members. Although organizations may have anti-discrimination initiatives they still expect non-majority employees in different jobs and levels, to adhere to the norms and values of the majority group. A pluralistic organization is one that simply contains many diverse groups of employees.

3. **Multicultural organizations** are more different still in that they value this diversity. In contrast to the assimilation approach practiced by monolithic and pluralistic organizations, they respond to employee differences by encouraging members of different groups to adopt some of the norms and values of other groups. A multicultural approach promotes appreciation of differences associated with the heritage,

characteristics, and values of members of different groups as well as respecting the uniqueness of each individual.

SUMMARY

This resource book does not assume that diversity and equality consultants are familiar with organizational theory. However, it is incumbent on users of this resource book to adopt the exercise accordingly with a view to ensuring they are have a good understanding of the relevant theories behind each exercise, in that their clients can benefit by ensuring that learning aims and objectives are achieved.

SECTION ONE:

PREJUDICE AND DISCRIMINATION

ORIGINS OF DIFFERENCE

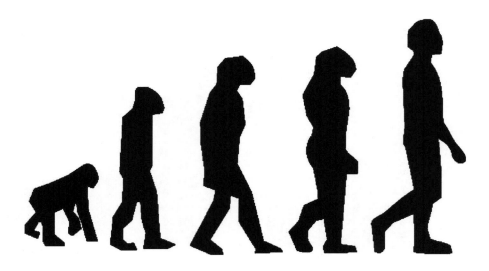

Aim	To recognize when we became aware of difference
Group Size	10 participants
Materials	Paper, Marker, Equality Questionnaire
Duration	30 Minutes

In this simple exercise, the leader facilitates a discussion based on one of the questions:

To do this successfully, a few ground rules are needed:

First, everyone is to talk about their own personal experience.

Equality Questionnaire

1. When did you first become aware of differences between the sexes?

2. When did you first become aware of differences in race?

3. When did you first become aware of differences in sexualities?

4. When did you first become aware of differences in class?

5. When did you first become aware of differences in abilities in people?

Extra Notes

1. The point of the exercise is not to necessarily talk about attitudes or prejudices toward groups—although those may come up--but to just recognize when we became aware of difference.

2. The moment may be first hand, when a participant saw and recognized someone different than themselves, or second hand, by overhearing a conversation, watching people in film or on TV.

3. If participants can't remember the earliest time, just ask them to tell of a time they remember when they were aware of the difference.

   After, discuss how the exercise made them feel or think—had they considered how they learned about difference before? How was it listening to other's histories?

PREJUDICE IN DAILY LIFE

Aim   To help participants connect prejudice and social justice to everyday activities and choices.

.

Group Size   10-40

Material   The template, markers and free space in which the participants can speak in small groups.

20 Minutes

Duration

Activity

After participants have read the "Making Connections" section of Understanding Prejudice and Discrimination (or other readings on environmental justice and the philosophy of interbeing), introduce this activity as follows:

"Just as categorical thinking can lead to prejudice and stereotyping, it can also lead us to view prejudice itself as being categorically distinct from the rest of life.

As Martin Luther King, Jr., and others have pointed out, however, prejudice and social justice are deeply intertwined in almost everything we do. Because this principle can sound abstract, let's look at a few concrete examples of how two seemingly unrelated things are actually closely connected."

Next, challenge participants to see how prejudice and inequality are connected to various mundane activities such as:

Wasting energy or consuming unnecessary plastic products [Possible answer based on environmental justice research: petrochemical industries disproportionately harm people of colour.]

Driving to work each day [Possible answers: (1) unnecessary driving and fuel inefficient cars waste petrochemicals; (2) luxury cars maintain social inequities]

Eating breakfast in the morning [Possible answers: (1) products such as coffee and cocoa often come from poor countries; (2) bacon and eggs inflict unnecessary harm on animals]

Bottom line: To think categorically of wasting energy as a strictly "environmental" issue is to miss the interconnectedness of the problem. From the framework of interbeing, working to protect the environment is also working to protect people of colour.

Caveat

Some participants may object to such connections, arguing that if prejudice were so embedded in daily life, they wouldn't be able to get through the day without worrying about how every little thing relates to prejudice. If these reactions surface, here are some points for participants to consider:

Often, it is uncomfortable to relate prejudice and inequality to our own lifestyles, and it cuts against the grain of our natural tendency to think categorically. Yet this discomfort does not make such an analysis wrong. A recognition of interconnectedness need not imply a net loss -- it can also be seen as a gain because working on one environmental or social justice issue is ultimately to work on all issues.

Viewed within this framework, prejudice reduction becomes a natural vehicle for self-improvement rather than a sacrifice or act of charity toward disadvantaged groups.

The philosophy of interbeing suggests that prejudice and inequality will never be eliminated entirely, but this need not be a problem. A quote from Thich Nhat Hanh is instructive in this regard:

"The problem is whether we are determined to go in the direction of compassion or not. If we are, then can we reduce the suffering to a minimum? If I lose my direction, I have to look for the North Star, and I go to the north. That does not mean I expect to arrive at the North Star. I just want to go in that direction." (Being Peace, p. 98)

DEMONSTRATING OBEDIENCE

Aim	To show that people do obey orders despite knowing better.
Group Size	10-40
Materials	List of request.
Duration	20 Minutes

PREPARATION

Prior to discussing obedience and the Milgram studies, you should enter the classroom and make sure that everyone is seated. Then go through a series of increasingly bizarre requests with your participants. Examples of possible requests are given below (feel free to substitute or add your own ideas here):

1. Ask participants to switch seats with another student

2. Have everyone remove their shoes and place them in a pile at the front of the room

3. Ask participants to take off their watch and exchange it with one other person

4. Ask participants to do jumping jacks in order to loosen up

5. Ask participants to rub their tummy while patting their head (and vice-versa)

6. Ask participants to do the wave (this one is actually very neat in a large class)

7. Ask participants to quack like a duck or to sing a silly song

8. Ask participants to come up with a class cheer (e.g., "we've got spirit yes we do, we've got spirit how 'bout you?") and yell it in unison several times as loud as they can.

9. End your session with a big round of applause, and then, after everyone has returned to their seat, ask them why they complied with the sequence of behaviours you requested of them.

10. Once participants recognize that they responded to requests made by an authority figure (i.e., because you are the professor),

11. Focusing the discussion on issues such as attributes of authority figures, why we obey authority, whether we should always obey authority, how a person gets authority, and what society would be like without authority.

12. This exercise is a real crowd-pleaser; besides being invigorating and entertaining, it helps participants relate the seemingly unreal circumstances of the Milgram experiment to their own real-life experiences.

13. It also tends to cure the "i would never obey an authority without good reason" feeling that participants often have when hearing about Milgram's results for the first time.

DEMONSTRATING OBEDIENCE

Obedience is a form of social influence where an individual acts in response to a direct order from another individual, who is usually an authority figure. It is assumed that without such an order the person would not have acted in this way. Obedience occurs when you are told to do something (authority), whereas conformity happens through social pressure (the norms of the majority). Obedience involves a hierarchy of power / status. Therefore, the person giving the order has a higher status than the person receiving the order.

The Milgram experiment on obedience to authority figures was a series of social psychology experiments conducted by Yale University psychologist Stanley Milgram, which measured the willingness of study participants to obey an authority figure who instructed them to perform acts that conflicted with their personal conscience.

Milgram found that subjects were more likely to obey in some circumstances than others. Obedience was highest when:

a) Commands were given by an authority figure rather than another volunteer.
b) The experiments were done at a prestigious institution
c) The authority figure was present in the room with the subject
d) The learner was in another room.
e) The subject did not see other subjects disobeying commands.

In everyday situations, people obey orders because they want to get rewards, because they want to avoid the negative consequences of disobeying, and because they believe an authority is legitimate. In more extreme situations, people obey even when they are required to violate their own values or commit crimes. Researchers think several factors cause people to carry obedience to extremes:

a) People justify their behaviour by assigning responsibility to the authority rather than themselves.

b) People define the behaviour that's expected of them as routine.

c) People don't want to be rude or offend the authority.

d) People obey easy commands first and then feel compelled to obey more and more difficult commands. This process is called entrapment, and it illustrates the foot-in-the-door phenomenon.

WHAT IS A MINORITY?

Aim	Creating a common understanding about the term minority. Promoting sharing among the participants.
Group Size	20-30 participants
Materials	Pens and paper
Duration	20 Minutes

DESCRIPTION

1. Each person writes down 4 characteristics, which can together define the concept of minority. The participants then go together in groups of three and share their 4 characteristics.

2. In case they have chosen different words, they negotiate until they reach an agreement of only 4 words. Now they go into groups of six and do the same. Eventually the whole group comes together.

3. At the end the group presents their common "definition" of minority.

Reflection

1. What are minorities?

2. What are ethnic minorities?

3. How do you become a minority?

4. How do you stop being a minority?

5. How can you change your minority status?

6. Does being a minority mean being disadvantaged?

7. Which kinds of discrimination can you fight through legislation?

8. Which limitations does legislation have?

WHAT IS MINORITY?

What is a minority? Creating a common understanding about the term minority. Promoting sharing among the participants. The term "minority group" often occurs alongside a discourse of civil rights and collective rights which gained prominence in the 20th century. Members of minority groups are prone to different treatment in the countries and societies in which they live. **Sociological minority** is not necessarily a numerical minority — it may include any group that is disadvantaged with respect to a dominant group in terms of social status, education, employment, wealth and political power.

Racial or ethnic minorities

Every large society contains ethnic minorities. They may be migrant, indigenous or landless nomadic communities. In some places, subordinate ethnic groups may constitute a numerical majority, such as Blacks in South Africa under apartheid.

Religious minorities

Most countries of the world have religious minorities. It is now widely accepted that people should have the freedom to choose their own religion, including not having any religion (atheism or agnosticism), and including the right to convert from one religion to another.

Gender Variant Minorities

In addition, various gender variant people can be seen as constituting a minority group or groups, such as intersexuals, transsexuals, and gender nonconformists — especially when such phenomena are understood as intrinsic characteristics of an identifiable group.

LGBT Minorities

The acronym LGBT is currently used to group these identities together.

The phrase sexual minorities can also be used to refer to these groups, and in addition may include fetishists, practitioner's gay, of BDSM, polyamorists and people who prefer sex partners of a disparate age.

Age Minorities

The elderly, while traditionally influential or even (in a gerontocracy) dominant in the past, have in the modern age usually been reduced to the minority role of economically 'non-active' groups. Children are a minority group in these terms, and the discrimination faced by the young is known as adultism. Discrimination against the elderly is known as ageism.

Disabled Minorities

The Disability rights movement consider standing of disabled people as a minority or a coalition of minorities who are disadvantaged by society, not just as people who are disadvantaged by their impairments.

IT'S THEIR FAULT!

Aim   To analyse how we discriminate against certain social groups and at the same time blame them for the situation they are in.

Group Size   Maximum 40. You will need to divide participants into four subgroups.

Materials   4 large sheets of paper; 4 old magazines; 4 scissors; 4 packs of coloured felt tip pens; 4 tubes of glue

Optional:

> 4 sets of other bits and pieces e.g. string,
> wool, buttons, paper clips. Paper and pen
> for the observers Clock or watch

Duration   20 Minutes.

Instructions:

1. Divide the players into four groups and ask each group to sit in a corner of the room where they can work comfortably.

2. The four groups should be quite far away from each other, so that they cannot hear each other well.

3. Ask each group to nominate one person to be an observer to note down what the members of the group do or say.

4. Announce that you will be coming round to each group in turn to give them the materials and the instructions of what to do.

5. Go to the first group, give them a set of materials and say clearly, 'You have a sheet of paper, a magazine, scissors and glue.

6. You must make a collage representing **Spring**. You have **20 minutes**. You may start whenever you want.' Then go to the second group, give them a set of materials and say clearly, 'You have a sheet of paper, a magazine, scissors and glue.

7. You must make a collage representing **Summer**. You have **20 minutes**. You may start whenever you want.' Then go to the third group, give them their materials and say clearly, 'You have a sheet of paper, a magazine, scissors and glue.

8. You must make a collage representing **Autumn**. You have **20 minutes**. You may start whenever you want.' Then go to the last group, give them their materials and say clearly, 'Mso, flosamd loerabtbz losnise bauqvxa poyeks,nseioamans sajiyudo laverza losifalitome. You have **20 minutes** to do it.

9. You may start whenever you want.' While the groups are working, go round the groups, be encouraging and supportive to the first, second and third groups, but blame the fourth group for not doing what you asked them to.

10. After **20 minutes** stop the activity and ask the groups to hand in their collages. If the first group has not yet finished give them 3 or 4 minutes more.

Evaluation

1. Start with a round from those who played. Ask them to say how they felt about the activity and how they worked together in their groups, did everyone participate?

2. Follow with a round from the observers. Ask them to say what happened in each group. If the fourth group received no help from the others, you may wish to ask why.

Then involve everybody in a discussion about the links with reality:

1. Can you see any links with real life?

2. In our society, who is in the fourth group?

3. How do we tend to blame the victims of social injustice?

4. How do people who feel they are the victims of social injustice react?

5. Do they react the same way as the people in group 4 did?

IT'S THEIR FAULT!

It's their fault: To analyse how we discriminate against certain social groups and at the same time blame them for the situation they are in.

Typology of Victims

The following is an attempt, based partly on Mendelson's original formulation, to classify victims according to their relative degree of responsibility and power to control or affect situations. These categories also judge the degree of guilt or responsibility, ranging from total innocence/no guilt, to 100% responsibility /total guilt.

Non guilty- innocent victim:

This category includes victims who do not share the responsibility of the offence with the perpetrators. These are innocent victims whom we cannot expect to be able to avert the offence by anticipating it or by preventing it.

Victims with Minor Guilt:

This category includes victims who with some thought, planning, awareness, information, or consciousness could have expected danger and avoided or minimized the harm to themselves. They 'could or should have known better.'

Victims who share equal responsibility with the perpetrators:

This category includes victims who share equal responsibility with the offender for the harm inflicted on them. These are people who are conscious and aware of the situation and chose to be part of it. They are not caught by surprise, and common sense could have anticipated the damage that occurred.

Victims who are exclusively responsible for their victimization:
This category includes victims who initiated the contact and committed an act that is likely to lead to injury. In these cases, the one who inflicts the damage is not guilty and acts in pure self-defence or as expected from his position. This category is reserved for legally and clinically sane adults.

The **above categories** represent an attempt to differentiate among many situations of victimhood. They comprise a controversial, inconclusive, and incomplete grid to determine guilt or responsibility. Demographic, cultural, and personal variables, while not accounted for in the above categories, are nevertheless crucial for the assessment of guilt and responsibility.

When evaluating the degree of responsibility, the following parameters must be also included:

- **Ethnicity** (minorities are more disposed to victimization than those in the majority),
- **Gender** (women are more disposed to victimization than men), socio-economic status (poor vs. rich),

- **Physical attributes** (less attractive, weak vs. more attractive, strong),

- **Mental status** (mentally ill, dysfunctional vs. healthy, functional),

- **Familial background** (abused, neglected vs. loved, nurtured), cultural values (cultures that promote violence vs. those that promote harmony).

Different kinds of multiple discrimination

Before this phenomenon can be adequately addressed it is necessary to have an adequate description of the different problems of multiple discrimination that can occur.

Multiple discrimination is said to occur when someone experiences discrimination on more than one ground, for instance, by being treated less favourably not only on grounds of race but also because of gender or disability. It is now accepted that there are broadly three ways in which multiple discrimination may manifest itself.

Firstly, **sequential discrimination** can occur when someone experiences discrimination on different grounds but on separate occasions. For example, a black woman may be passed over for promotion because, firstly, her employers want a man to take the lead, and then, on another occasion, she may be excluded because of her skin colour. Here the current EU laws are likely to be adequate, since it is a single aspect of her multiple identity that is relevant to each occasion.

Secondly, **additive discrimination** can occur where requirements are cumulative, for instance, a series of desired attributes are stated in a job description, so that the lack of one merely decreases the chance of success in getting the job, but the lack of a further characteristic will additionally decrease the chance of success. The case of Perera v Civil Service Commission (no 2) provides an example of this kind of approach.

In this case, the employer set out a series of requirements for a potential post-holder. Mr Perera was turned down for the job due to a variety of desired attributes he was assessed by the interviewing committee as being unable to fulfil, namely: experience in the UK, the command of English, nationality and age. Here, the lack of one attribute did not prevent him getting the job but it did make it less likely. Unable to show that he had two such attributes further decreased his chance of selection. So ultimately he was unsuccessful on a variety of different grounds. In cases of 'additive discrimination' the steps in the overall treatment can be analysed separately and can consequently usually be adequately addressed.

Multiple discrimination has been widely recognized for some time by those working in the equality field as a problem that must be addressed. Yet creating appropriate legal and policy responses to disadvantage based on a variety of grounds has proved difficult. Historically, different approaches to different grounds have developed in an ad hoc way in response to a variety of single focus campaigns without the consistency and coherence that would ideally underpin an effective equality law.

A deeper understanding of the complexity of the many ways in which discrimination operates in practice in society has led to a greater awareness of the operation of multiple discrimination.

I HAVE A DREAM

Aim   To strengthen feelings of equality within the group through the sharing of dreams and visions.

Group Size   6-40 Participants

Materials	Flipchart, Marker, Paper
Duration	60 minutes

Instructions:

1. How you organise this activity will depend on the size of your group. If it is a medium-size group, do it as a whole group, if the group is large, divide people up into small groups of 5-6?

2. Tell them to spend the first five minutes reflecting on their own, how they would like things to be in the future – in terms of family, job, hobbies, housing, personal development, civil rights, etc.

3. Then ask people to share their dreams and aspirations saying what they are and giving reasons. They should write down, or preferably draw, any common features on a large piece of paper e.g. having a job, travelling, having children, their own house, etc. and give reasons.

4. Ask each group to present their drawings or conclusions to the plenary.

5. Continue by asking people individually or in groups to identify three concrete things that prevent them from pursuing their aspirations, and three concrete things that they, as a group(or an organisation), can do to get closer seeing their dreams come true.

Debriefing and evaluation

Start by asking people to share the feelings they experienced while doing this activity and then to say what they enjoyed about the exercise.

Follow with other questions:

1. Was there anything that surprised you?
2. Do you think that everybody should have the right to pursue their aspirations?
3. Do you feel that some people may have more chances than others?
4. Who and why and is it fair?
5. How can you support each other in practical ways to overcome the barriers and make your dreams come true?

I HAVE A DREAM

The theory behind this exercise is that the vision of equality has always been important for oppressed and under-represented minority groups, who often express their concerns regarding unfairness and inequality, by way of violent and non-violent means.

The Personal Mission Statement

1. **Personal Vision**: outlines what the individual wants to be, and how they want the world in which they operate to see them. It is a long-term view and concentrates on the future.

2. **Personal Mission:** Defines the fundamental purpose of an individual, which succinctly describes what they need to do in order to achieve their vision.

3. **Personal Values**: Beliefs that are shared among individuals whose values are linked to organizations, which share their values, culture and priorities.

4. **Personal Strategy**: Strategy, narrowly defined is a combination of end goals and the means of achieving them.

5. The most important part of implementing the strategy is ensuring the company is going in the right direction - defined as towards the end vision

Further Information

Dominant and ruling social groups may also feel threatened or under pressure, because oppressed and the minority groups have vision of equality that they also considered unfair, because in their eyes oppressed and minority groups have visions and dreams of equality that threaten their status quo.

The GROW model can be used to achieve the equality and diversity visions aspiration and dreams vision in the following manner.

- **Goal:**   The goal is usually the end point; it's the place where the individuals or groups of people visualize an end to oppression or under-representation.

- **Reality:** The current reality is that individuals and groups of individuals continue to face the challenge of under-representation, discrimination and prejudice, thus delaying the realization of their diversity and equality goals.

- **Obstacles:** There will be diversity and equality obstacles stopping individuals groups such as institutional and individual prejudice, if there were no obstacles, individual and groups facing discrimination would already have reached their goals.

- **Option**s: Once obstacles have been identified, individuals need to find ways of dealing with them, if they are to make progress.

- **Way Forward:** The Options then need to be converted into action steps which will take the client to their goal. These are the Way.

DEMONSTRATING GROUP POLARIZATION

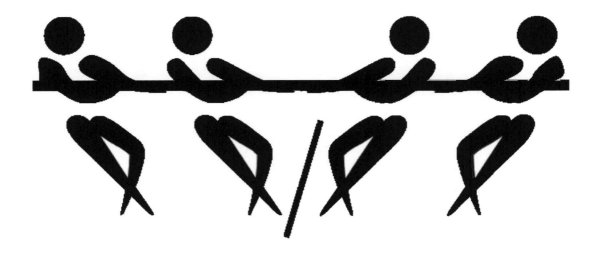

Aim	To demonstrate the group polarization effect
Group Size	10
Materials	Paper, Pen, Likert Scale
Duration	20 Minutes

Instructions

As part of a group decision exercise, ask participants to declare on a Likert scale how strongly they agree or disagree with some statement or idea.

First Stage

1. Obama care should be scrapped

2. Affirmative action works

3. Racial prejudice and discrimination no longer exists.

4. Any Black-White differences in economic outcomes is a result of Black people's lack of motivation to work hard.

5. Black people's anger over inequality is unjustified since they are unwilling to work to get what they want.

6. Black people seek special favours rather than working to get ahead.

7. Relative to White people, Black people have been getting more economically than they deserve.

Second Stage

1. Collect the responses and divide participants into like-minded groups for a short, 5-minute discussion.

2. After the group discussion, have participants rate their agreement with the proposition again on the same Likert scale.

3. The results should be consistent with group polarization: those who initially agreed should agree more strongly after group discussion, and those who initially disagreed should disagree even more strongly after group discussion.

DEMONSTRATING GROUP POLARIZATION

Group polarization is the phenomenon that when placed in group situations, people will make decisions and form opinions to more of an extreme than when they are in individual situations. The phenomenon has shown that after participating in a discussion group, members tend to advocate more extreme positions and call for riskier courses of action than individuals who did not participate in any such discussion. The importance of group polarization is significant as it helps explain group behaviour in a variety of real-life situations. Examples of these situations include public policy, terrorism, the vote, affirmative action, the death penalty, gun ownership, abortion, jury decisions

In 1970, Myers and Bishop selected groups of highly racially prejudiced participants and groups of less racially prejudiced participants to discuss a number of racial issues. Results demonstrated that racial prejudice decreased for already low-prejudice individuals and increased for already high-prejudice individuals after individuals engaged in their respective group discussion. Thus, their study supported the claim that discussion among like-minded individuals tends to increase and intensify pre-existing attitudes, thereby demonstrating group polarization.

Moreover, in recent years, the Internet and online social media have also presented opportunities to observe group polarization and compile new research. Psychologists have found that social media outlets such as Facebook and Twitter demonstrate that group polarization can occur even when a group is not physically together. As long as the group of individuals begins with the same fundamental opinion on the topic and a consistent dialogue is kept going, group polarization can be observed.

In 2010, Sarita and Boyd analyzed 30,000 tweets on Twitter regarding the shooting of George Tiller, a late term abortion doctor. The tweets analyzed were conversations among pro-life and pro-choice advocates post shooting. They found that like-minded individuals strengthen group identity whereas replies between different-minded individuals reinforce a split in affiliation. This showed that people will group together based on opinions and polarize in one direction no matter what their location is.

The results should be consistent with group polarization: those who initially agreed should agree more strongly after group discussion, and those who initially disagreed should disagree even more strongly after group discussion. According to Gray, asking your participants to speculate about the causes of the effect should generate the same explanations generated by psychologists over the years (i.e., that members are exposed to new, persuasive arguments, and that members gradually take a more extreme position in order to be viewed positively by others). An added benefit is that, in addition to learning the group polarization effect in a memorable way, participants learn that they can successfully "think like psychologists" in generating plausible explanations for observed events.

References

Aronson, Elliot (2010). Social Psychology. Upper Saddle River, NJ: Prentice Hall. p. 273.

Myers, D.G.; H. Lamm (1975). "The polarizing effect of group discussion". American Scientist 63 (3): 297–303. Bibcode:1975AmSci..63..297M. PMID 1147368.

Bray, R. M.; A. M. Noble (1978). "Authoritarianism and decisions of mock juries: Evidence of jury bias and group polarization". Journal of Personality and Social Psychology 36 (12): 1424–1430. doi:10.1037/0022-3514.36.12.1424.

Tips for the facilitator

1. If you are working with just a few people adapt the game and create two sub-groups, the first with very clear instructions and the second with confusing ones.

2. An alternative to using the nonsense sentence with the fourth group is to give them proper instructions spoken very fast or in another language.

3. Depending on the group, you may wish to choose other themes for the collages, especially if you feel that the series of seasons would be too easy for the fourth group to follow.

4. Be aware that this activity is likely to generate strong reactions from the members of the fourth group because of the frustration of not understanding the instructions and still being blamed for it.

5. Sometimes they get angry with the facilitator and leave; sometimes they turn their frustration against the other groups and prevent them from doing or finishing their work; sometimes they withhold their feelings and keep their aggression for later.

SECTION TWO:

THE ROLE OF MEDIA SECTION

LEMONS

Aim	This is an icebreaker which introduces the idea of individual differences. It can be used at the start of a session around stereotyping, differences and equality of opportunities
Group Size	Any size
Materials	Enough lemons for everybody in the group ,A carrier bag
Duration	30 minutes

Instruction:

1. Give each group member a lemon.

2. Ask everyone to look closely at their fruit, examine it for distinctive marks and feel the skin.

3. Encourage each person to personalise their lemon by giving it a name.

4. Allow five minutes to do this and then collect all the lemons into the carrier bag. Shake the bag to mix the fruits.

5. Spread all the lemons out on the floor in front of the group.

6. In turn, ask each young person to come forward and collect their lemon.

7. If there is an argument over whose it is, try to adjudicate, but if they still can't agree, place the lemon to one side as unidentified.

8. If this happens, you should be left with two at the end to reunite, but will find that most people (amazingly!) can successfully claim their fruit.

Reflection and Evaluation:

1. Once all the young people have been reunited with their lemons you can facilitate a discussion.

2. How sure are they that they claimed the right fruit?

3. How can they tell?

4. Encourage them to look at the parallels between this exercise and differentiating between people.

Examine the stereotypes:

1. Are all lemons the same colour?

2. Are they all the same shape?

3. Reflect this into the stereotypes that exist between people of different cultures, races and gender.

4. What does this mean to the group?

Objectives:

1. Participants will be able to define stereotype.

2. Participants will be able to recognize the role media, peers, and family play in teaching stereotypes.

3. Participants will be able to identify various types of stereotypes.

4. Participants will identify some possible impacts of stereotyping on both those who are stereotyped and those doing the stereotyping.

5. Participants will be able to identify ways to challenge or eliminate stereotypes

LEMONS

1. This is an icebreaker which introduces the idea of individual differences. It can be used at the start of a session around stereotyping, differences and equality of opportunities. We all have stereotypes and it's important we are aware of what they are in order to begin challenging them in others and ourselves.

2. **Stereotypes** are learned attitudes that have significant impact on our behaviours. We learn them from a variety of sources including television, books, music, our peers, families, etc.

3. **Stereotypes** are generalizations made about a group of people e that are usually based on inaccurate or incomplete information. They can be **positive or negative**, but both can have negative consequences for the person or people being stereotyped.   Whenever we stereotype someone, we are ignoring them as individuals and lumping the whole group together as "they are all like that." Stereotypes can be very difficult to change.

4. **Stereotype**s happen when we judge people from our own frame of reference or our own cultural expectations about how people should look, behave, talk, etc.

GENDER STEREOTYPES
IN ADVERTISING

Aim

To understand the implications of stereotyped thinking

Group Size

Any size

Materials

Newsprint and markers or flip chart; one index card for each participant; container (such as a paper sack, shoebox, or hat); pens/pencils

Duration   30-40 minutes

Instructions

1. Ask Participant to discuss or list the role of advertisements in the development and perpetuation of gender-role stereotypes

2. Using the types of stereotyping listed above, you need to find a set of advertisements that illustrate one or more of the types and preferably have them made into slides (or, if your class is relatively small, you can make photocopied packets of the ads and use them in future classes).

3. You can also include advertisements that illustrate non-traditional or innovative gender-role portrayals as well as ads that do not incorporate gender stereotypes at all.

4. Use Goffman's types of gender stereotyping (it is best to write them on the board) and provide sample advertisements, ask participants to take out a blank sheet of paper and number it from 1 to 20.

5. Tell participants that you are going to show them a series of 20 advertisements, and they are to indicate which types of gender stereotyping, if any, are depicted in each ad.

6. After showing the advertisements, go over them and discuss participants' responses to each. Jones suggested that class discussion can focus on how advertisements influence gender stereotypes as well as changes in stereotypes over time (if you included advertisements from the 1950s), and how other sources (such as television or the workplace) contribute to gender stereotyping.

GENDER STEREOTYPES IN ADVERTISING

It is argued, that adverts are teaching viewers a vast array of social cues, and even the most subtle ones make an impact on the viewers. Furthermore, it is said that gender relations are learned through advertisements. Among these learned gender roles are those of femininity and masculinity. Men and women are portrayed in advertisements according to the constructed definition of femininity and masculinity. To be a woman is to be feminine and to be a man is to be masculine. There is little room for variation or a reversal of roles, except within the smaller frame of: niche marketing.

You might also explore with your participants the role advertisements play in the development and perpetuation of gender-role stereotypes. Jones (1991) noted that an analysis of advertisements by Goffman (1976) found numerous instances of subtle stereotyping including:

1. **Functional ranking** — the tendency to depict men in executive roles and as more functional when collaborating with women.

2. **Relative size** — the tendency to depict men as taller and larger than women, except when women are clearly superior in social status.

3. **Ritualization of subordination** — an overabundance of images of women lying on floors and beds or as objects of men's mock assaults.

4. **The feminine touch** — the tendency to show women cradling and caressing the surface of objects with their fingers.

5. **Family** — fathers depicted as physically distant from their families or as relating primarily to sons, and mothers depicted as relating primarily to daughters.

THE PORTRAYAL OF MEN IN ADVERTISING:

- Alert and conscious of surroundings
- Standing upright
- Eyes open and looking around
- Bodies are controlled
- Mean expression on face
- Gripping things tightly with hands
- Hands in pockets
- Serious
- Physically active

Bravery, adventurousness, being able to think rationally, being strong and effective, for example, are all "manly" traits that are usually encouraged. So is the ability to think independently and take the initiative. Media images supporting these behaviours include the strong, silent Marlboro man and military ads telling young men to be 'all you can be'.

THE PORTRAYAL OF WOMEN IN ADVERTISING:

- Touching self
- Caressing an object
- Lying on the floor
- Sitting on a bed or chair
- Eyes closed
- Not alert

- Confused
- Vulnerable
- Body contorted
- Dressed like a child
- Holding an object or a man for support
- Sexy and sexually available
- Seductive
- Playful

Women are often portrayed in positions of submissiveness and powerlessness. This can be clearly seen when women are shown lying on the floor as men are standing over them, literally depicting women as being beneath men. Women are urged to pursue beauty and sex appeal, and part of the sex appeal is submission. The body – and particularly here the female body – is always inevitably controlled by social norms and the commodification of the body through industries such as fashion and beauty that exhibit femininity.

BODY IMAGE AND SEXUALITY IN ADVERTISING

Since the 1980s, men's bodies have been used more for advertising, depicting a similarly idealized body image to that portrayed of women further; a growing number of advertisements are showing men as sex objects. A study on male body obsession found that advertisements for everything from cars to underwear depicted body-builder images with "washboard abdominal muscles, massive chests, and inflated shoulders. Though women's equality is advancing in society, men have become more fixated with muscularity because it is still seen as a cultural symbol of masculinity. In addition, it has been suggested that a muscular body has become an aesthetic norm for heterosexuals as well as homosexuals.

In a content analysis study of exclusively male images in men's magazines, it was found that most of the bodies in advertising were not 'ordinary', but those of strong and hard 'male figures'. The study showed that males in the advertisements were usually objectified and depersonalized. The representation of ectomorphs (thin and lightly muscled) was limited predominantly to the advertising of clothing that may look more appealing on slimmer, taller men. Endomorphs (soft and round) were rarely depicted and if they were, tended to be the object of humour. It is important to note that representations of male bodies are often used irrespective of their relevance to the product being promoted in advertising; men are often portrayed in the following ways:

References:

Baran, Stanley J.; Dennis K. Davis (2008). Mass communication theory: foundations, ferment, and future. Cengage Learning. p. 318. ISBN 0-495-50363-0.

Belknap, Penny; William Leonard II. "A Conceptual Replication and Extension of Erving Goffman' s Study of Gender Advertisements". Retrieved 4 December 2011.

Elliott, R. and C. Elliott (2005). "Idealized images of the male body in advertising: a reader-response exploration."

Goffman, Erving. "ERVING GOFFMAN & GENDER ADVERTISEMENTS".

Jhally, Sut. "The Codes of Gender". Media Education Foundation. .

MEDIA PORTRAYALS

Purpose

This activity enables participants to analyze the ways in which different populations are portrayed in the media, and within different forms of the media, to determine what images exist, to compare these portrayals with reality, and to discuss the positive versus negative portrayals, as well as implications of exposure to these images.

Time: 10 Minutes

Materials: Newspapers, Music videos

Procedure

1. Ask participants to review a given number of media presentations pertaining to a given population.

2. You might request that they only discuss those in which that population is represented, or you could ask them to review media to determine the prevalence of images for that population.

3. Ask them to explain whether or not the images are generally positive or negative and whether or not any patterns emerge with regard to these images. For example, are older women more likely to be portrayed negatively than older men? Or, you might ask them to determine if certain television stations depict certain groups more positively than others.

4. Now, ask the participants to discuss the implications of such media presentations in terms of the socialization of children and others.

5. Do children and adults formulate negative perceptions of others as a result of these images?

6. Do these images serve to support racist/sexist/classist, etc. ideologies? In other words, how alike is group A and group B?

7. You can ask that participants do this project alone or in groups and either as a written project or an in-class discussion (although the latter requires more time and preparation on your part -- bringing in magazines for them to look through, etc.).

8. This exercise can be used in a number of ways and with any type of media. In addition, it might be modified for use in any number of courses

9. For example, the activity might be used in a communications course to discuss the impact of mass media on perceptions of populations within a diverse population and the representativeness of the mass media in the images it portrays.

MEDIA PORTRAYALS

Media Portrayals: This activity enables participants to analyze the ways in which different populations are portrayed in the media, and within different forms of the media, to determine what images exist, to compare these portrayals with reality, and to discuss the positive versus negative portrayals, as well as implications of exposure to these images.

1. **Lady and the Tramp** there are Siamese cats which are characters. They are supposed to represent **Asians** and they have certain stereotypical physical characteristics such as slanted eyes and they also have a strong accent. Also the song they are in has Chinese music in the background. In the movie Cinderella there is a stepmother and stepsisters. They are very mean and harsh to Cinderella and it stereotypes stepmothers and stepsisters as people who are evil.

2. **Rush Hour** Jackie Chan is Chinese and he knows how to fight with martial arts. He also loves to eat Chinese food. Chris Tucker is also in the movie and he is black. He is shown in the movie to love listening to rap music. He is also shown as loving fried chicken. This stereotypes that African Americans love to eat chicken and listen to rap.

3. **Harold and Kumar movies**: The man Kumar, who is played by Kal Penn, is and Indian. He is told by his father to become a surgeon and both Kumar and Harold are very smart. This stereotypes that Indians usually become doctors and that Asians are supposed to be really smart. In the Harold and Kumar movies, there is a scene where they are on a plane going to Amsterdam. On the plane there is an old lady that sees Kumar as a sort of Arabic man with a turban and a long beard and she screams terrorist. This stereotypes that people from the Middle East are terrorists.

4. **Hancoc**k there is a scene where Will Smith who is the main actor tries to buy alcohol from a small store. The owner of the store is an Indian man which stereotypes that the owners of 7-11 type stores are usually Indian.**Fantasia 2000**, they show a servant to white person and the servant is black. Also in the movie Jungle Book, nearly all of the characters speak very proper English, however the monkeys which are portrayed as lazy and good for nothing speak in more of a black accent

5. **Dumbo** there is a group of crows which sing a song when they hear that an elephant can fly. They are black crows and they also talk in black accents. The crows in the movie are seen as loud and ignorant, to the point that they are even rude at times

MEDIA STEREOYPES

Aim	To e Explore media messages about diverse groups of people
Group Size	Any
Materials	Print and Magazine media, cable ,satellite TV
Duration	Session 1: 15 minutes to introduce; Session 2:30-40 minutes

Planning Notes:

Divide the group into six teams to do this activity. To prepare hand-outs for each small group, make six copies of the hand out and label them with one of the following:

a)   Women

b)   Old people

c)   African Americans

d)   Asians

e)   People with disabilities

f)   Lesbian, gay and bisexual people

1. Then, make enough copies of each labelled hand out so each team member has the same hand out.

2. For Step 4 you will need examples of media messages to help teens understand what to look for when they look critically at the media.

3. Two weeks or so before you plan to begin the activity, look for both print and electronic media images.

5. Watch television shows and movies popular with your group, and clip sample images from teen magazines and newspapers. (For example, you might share several contrasting visual images of women in the print media or your observations about the portrayal of African Americans in popular sitcoms or movies.)

4.

6. Some populations—lesbian, gay and bisexual people and people with disabilities—are largely absent from the popular media.

7. Groups assigned those populations will have a more difficult task. In Session 2, discuss which groups are not represented.

Procedure:

Session 1

1. Ask teens for examples of popular television shows (both network and cable), movies and magazines. List them on newsprint or the board, by category.

2. Ask teens how they would rate the portrayals - on a scale from O (very negative) to 10 (very positive) for their representation and treatment of diverse groups of people.

3. Explain that by "diversity" you mean people of colour, women, old people, people with disabilities, and lesbian, gay and bisexual people.

Take a quick assessment of the group's rankings and write them on the board or newsprint, under the following headings:

a)   Network television

b)   Cable television

c)   Movies

d)   Magazines

Tell participants to evaluate how the media portrays different groups of people that are discriminated against.

Go over instructions for the activity:

You will work in six teams and each team will be assigned one group of people to research in the media.

The groups we will research are:

a)   Women

b)   Old people

c)   People with disabilities

d)   Lesbian, gay and bisexual people

e)   Ethnic Minorities

1. Find at least two examples of how your group of people is portrayed in these four media: network and cable television, film and magazines.

2. Review television programs, movies and magazines.

3. Find examples and take notes on your hand-outs.

4. Bring your completed hand-outs and be prepared to share your findings with the whole group at the next session.

5. Divide participants into six groups and distribute to each the hand-outs you have prepared. Provide several examples of media messages to help the groups get started. Use different, contrasting types of images and discuss them briefly to be sure everyone understands what to do with their assignments.

Session 2

6. Invite the teams to make their presentations. Ask for a group to volunteer to go first.

7. Ask for their overall rating of how each medium treats their category of people and record it on the board or newsprint.

8. Repeat the process until all six groups have presented, then remind the group of the ratings they gave at the beginning of this activity.

9. Have them adjust their media ratings up or down, according to their research.

Conclude the activity using the discussion points.

10. .Overall, which medium does the best job of portraying diversity positively? Give examples of positive portrayals.

11. Which does the worst job? Give examples of offensive portrayals.

12. Do other media (such as newspapers, popular book, comic books, music videos, popular radio shows) portray diversity in a positive or negative light? Are particular groups portrayed better or worse than others?

MEDIA STEREOTYPES

Media Stereotypes: This exercise aims to explore media messages about diverse groups of people through television, programmes. It is understood that racism stereotypes are seen all around us in today's world. Of all the places that it is prevalent, it is probably seen most through the media. Movies which are meant to be entertainment can have many subtle meanings which impact the way people think.

The Simpsons? Homer Simpson is the biggest example of the American stereotype as perceived by the world. The common view is that Americans are obese, lazy, and dull, and Homer Simpson completely epitomizes this perception. However, it is ironic that his very own daughter Lisa is bright and intelligent, thereby countering the entire view immediately.

Another example of stereotyping in The Simpsons is that of the character Appu. Appu is an Indian, who is depicted as dark and talking with a heavy Indian accent. However, not all Indians are dark skinned, and not all of them have an accent associated with the English language. As you can see from these examples, all of them have what you may call a biased opinion towards a group, based on what has been seen or heard about them.

They racism and stereotypes can have a negative effect on people as they begin to believe what they see. The problem is not that they believe however. The problem is that what they start to accept at true is not always the case. Although we can try as hard as possible, the media is something that is unavoidable and will always impact our culture.

TELEVISION PREJUDICES

Aim	To demonstrate the prevalence of stereotypes and prejudice in the media
Group Size	Any size
Material	Television Prejudices: Logging Form" hand out, writing utensils .
Duration	30 minutes

Facilitator Instructions:

1. Distribute the "Television Prejudices: Logging Form" hand out.

2. Instruct participants to watch at least two television shows and one news program. These should be aired between the hours of 5:00 p.m. and 10:00 p.m.

3. Participants are to record the number of times that they hear a prejudicial remark or see a stereotype being depicted in each program.

4. The stereotypes should relate to race/ethnicity, religion, gender, sexual orientation, or age.

5. Participants are then to write about the feelings they experienced when they watched the programs and the importance of being aware of stereotypes.

6. When they turn in their assignments the next day, take about 20 minutes to ask the following questions:

7. What kinds of programs contained stereotypes and prejudiced language?

8. Comedies? Dramas? The news?

9. Which types of programs contained the most stereotypes and prejudicial language?

10. What groups of people did these shows stereotype?

11. Do you think it is acceptable for these programs to portray stereotypes and use prejudicial language?

12. Does it make a difference if the show is a comedy, a drama, or the news?

13. What effect do these shows have on our individual lives?

14. What effect do they have on society as a whole?

15. Do you think shows like this help or hurt people's ability to get along with and understand each other?

TELEVISION PREJUDICES CTD

The media is a business, and do what is necessary to gain viewers or readers. They produce stories that will appeal to the emotions and interests of the people. In addition, media has to deal with slow days twist stories to make them seem more interesting than they really are.

- **These media wheel of oppression** continues to transport a self-fulfilling prophecy of discrimination. The public sees and hears, and reads who is supposed to be smart or dumb, leader or follower, law abiding or criminal. It is discouraging to see how in large measure the public easily subscribes to these covert imagined directives of social order.

- **Media decision makers** are perhaps the descendants of families of Hollywood royalty- past and present media stars, producers, and powerful behind-the-scene figures that have historically profited from mistaken assumptions that traditional stereotypes sell product and sensational images are what the public wants to see.

- **Entertainment decision-maker assumptions** are silently rooted in familial underpinnings grounded in ethnocentric beliefs, norms, and values systems, which also serve a deeper psychological purpose.

- In large measure, stereotypic media portrayal positively reinforces the particular ethnic heritage and social prowess of **TV decision makers** in the existing system of influence, power, and control-at-large in the United States.

Reference:

Rada, J.A., &Wulfemeyer, K.T. (2005, March). Colour coded descriptors in television coverage of intercollegiate sports. Journal of Broadcasting & Electronic Media. 65(21). Retrieved March 10, 2008 from Gale database.

DIVERSITY NEWSPAPERS

Aim	• To help participants get to know each other better, establish openness
	• Encourage creative oral presentations and active listening skills
	• Stimulate awareness on different perspectives related to cultural diversity.
Group Size	Various small groups of three to five
Materials	Postcards, from examples given overleaf or your own devising, a bowl or cup

Duration   40 minutes

Instructions:

1. "Participants are placed in   pairs to realise a structured interview"

2. Interviews will then constitute the page of a (huge) newspaper that will be displayed on one of the training room walls and read by all participants.

3. **How you create pairs**: Place little pieces of paper in a bowl, half of them are blank, the others have the first name of half participants written on.

4. Ask each participant to pick one, then to identify who is the person he/she will interview or to wait for somebody to come and interview them (the case of those with blank pieces paper).

Instructions for the interview:

5. Each person interviews his/her partner (approx. 15-20 min per person) and writes the answers according to the given outline (see a template below).

6. Then interview-pairs swap roles, so that the interviewer becomes the one that provides information.

Structure for information to collect about the other

7. Personal information (name, nationality, place of residence, hobbies etc.)

8. Education where does he/she work (organisation, activities*) and what is his/her occupation (frame trainer role)

9. His/her favourite training topic (i.e., project management, conflict transformation)

1. A personal story illustrating the challenges related to cultural diversity that comes to his/her mind

2. If you have time (an extra half an hour) and it is useful for your session/course, each person could orally introduce his/her interview-partner (max. 1 minute each).

3. The interview papers are stuck on the wall in order to create a big Diversity newspaper. A scotch tape framing all A3 sheets and a title added gives a nice, cohesive image.

4. How to motivate the others to read the newspaper: give to each participant self-adhesive dots and ask them to stick the dots on the newspaper article that is most appealing to them.

DIVERSITY NEWSPAPERS

Diversity Newspapers: To have participants define for themselves the meaning of diversity. Media bias is the bias or perceived bias of journalists and news producers within the mass media in the selection of events and stories that are reported and how they are covered.

The term "media bias" implies a pervasive or widespread bias contravening the standards of journalism, rather than the perspective of an individual journalist or article. The direction and degree of media bias in various countries is widely disputed.

Practical limitations to media neutrality include the inability of journalists to report all available stories and facts, and the requirement that selected facts be linked into a coherent narrative.

Government influence, including overt and covert censorship, biases the media in some countries, for example North Korea and Burma.

Market forces that result in a biased presentation include the ownership of the news source, concentration of media ownership, the selection of staff, the preferences of an intended audience, and pressure from advertisers.

Types of bias

The most commonly discussed forms of bias occur when the media support or attack a particular political party, candidate, or ideology, but other common forms of bias include:

1. Advertising bias, when stories are selected or slanted to please advertisers.
2. Corporate bias, when stories are selected or slanted to please corporate owners of media.
3. Mainstream bias, a tendency to report what everyone else is reporting, and to avoid stories that will offend anyone.

4. **Sensationalism bias** in favour of the exceptional over the ordinary, giving the impression those rare events, such as airplane crashes are more common, than common events, such as automobile crashes.

5. **Concision bias**, a tendency to report views that can be summarized succinctly, crowding out more unconventional views that take time to explain.

Other forms of bias including reporting that favours or attacks a particular race, religion, gender., age, sexual orientation, ethnic group, or even person.

Gate keeping bias, i.e., deciding whether to release a story or keep it under wraps. (Coverage bias statement bias).

THE MUSIC STEREOTYPE

Aim Young people become aware of the effect of youth culture on a specific issue; and how a particular issue can be perceived by and affect other members of society.

Group Size   At least 10

Materials   Cassette of current/chart music and cassette player

                    Flipchart/stand and pens

Duration (5 minutes)

Description

1. Play the current chart/popular music tape in the background to encourage a 'going out' atmosphere. Draw an outline of person (non-gender specific) on the flipchart.

2. Ask the participants to close their eyes and soak up the music while you are doing this. Explain what will happen for the rest of the session, specifying that you will be creating and exploring the issue using a character

3. Ask everyone to close their eyes. Begin the story: 'Imagine…It's Saturday night, it's eight o'clock, and a young person is getting ready to go out. They have just got out of the shower and they are getting dressed. They are really looking forward to this evening.' Then start to say questions for them to think about concerning the character.

Questions could include:

a)   What is their name?

b)   Where are they going?

c)   What are they wearing?

d)   How old are they?

e)   Who are they going out with?

f)   Where do they live?

Step-by-step

1. Be careful to leave details to their imagination. Ask them to open eyes. Ask them to shout out answers to the questions and fill in the details on the picture – any other information, write down the side of the flipchart. **(10 minutes)**

2. Now you have built the character, continue with the story by placing the character in an emergency situation around your issue. For example, if your issue is drugs, the character may go to a nightclub and be offered a drug; if your issue is sexual health, the character may be going to a party to meet a new partner. Leave this open-ended and ask the group to complete the story by calling out what happened. Agree on the story. **(5 minutes)**

3. Now get the group to each imagine they know their character – ask them to say who they are and what their relationship is (for example, I am X's mother – I'm X's friend – I'm X's dog – I'm X's next door neighbour) and what their feelings/views of X are (for example, I'm X's

tutor. They are very likeable and lively. I've been worried about them lately…). **(10 minutes)**

4. Ask the group to form 'conscience alley'. Participants form a double row facing each other. Tutor takes role of X and walks through, facing each in turn. In their roles, each gives advice or comments to X on the situation. **(10 minutes)**

5. Afterwards de-role group – ask them, as themselves, to comment on X's behaviour. Identify the moment of decision. How could things have turned out differently? What were the risks/pressures? **(10 minutes)**

Reflection and evaluation:

Get them to review the character and situation: Was it realistic? Which bits are true or false? What about stereotypes? What should education for young people around this issue include to give a realistic reflection of youth culture? **(5 minutes)**

THE MUSIC STEREOTYPE

Music and Stereotypes: The aim of this exercise is to encourage participants to discuss how and why stereotypes began in music, while exploring why different groups take their music further than the headphones. Like, for example, in their clothing, if you happen to wear black jeans and a graphic tee of a band you like, people will probably look at you and consider that maybe you're a metal head. The same goes for people that wear cowboy boots and Carhartt coats. Yes, you probably guessed it, country music. The point is that the music influences the listener, which influences the style, which is then associated back to the music that originally sparked the style. This results in a stereotype! This exercise will encourage participants to be aware of the effect of youth culture on a specific issue and how a particular issue can be perceived by and affect other members of society. Numerous studies say about their sounds:

- **POP**: Conformists, overly responsible, role-conscious, and struggling with sexuality or peer acceptance.

- **HEAVY METAL**: Higher levels of suicidal ideation, depression, drug use, self-harm, shoplifting, vandalism, unprotected sex.

- **DANCE**: Higher levels of drug use regardless of socio-economic background.

- **JAZZ/RHYTHM & BLUES**: Introverted misfits, loners.

- **RAP**: Higher levels of theft, violence, anger, street gang membership, drug use and misogyny.

POLITICAL STEREOTYPES

Aim   Awareness of the misuse of the concept of culture to exclude ethnic minorities (with examples from the extreme right and mainstream media).

Group Size   8 – 32 (working in smaller groups of 4-8 persons)

Materials   Worksheets, flipchart, pens, the cases

Duration   90 minutes or more

Procedure

Split the participants into 4 groups. Each group will be given a case they have to discuss and then present in plenary. They will get a sheet with 1) a case & 2) some questions to discuss.

Part one (30 minutes)

The participants discuss the cases.

Part two (30 minutes)

In plenary each group is asked to present their case shortly

Part three: (20 minutes)

1. What can culture explain in connection to behaviour?
2. What can it not explain?
3. Which other explanations of the behaviour did you come up with?
4. What happens when we try to explain delinquency, unemployment etc. with the concept of culture?
5. When arguing that we should respect culture no matter what, what do we miss out on?

Debriefing: (10 minutes)

Sum up the debriefing with a presentation of stereotypes, prejudices, discrimination and exclusion. Be aware of cultural differences as a first best guess, but beware of the use of culture to explain or excuse negative behaviour. Otherwise culture turns into a new concept for "race".

POLITICAL STEREOTYPES

This exercise is about developing a greater awareness of the use of political stereotypes to exclude minorities Normally we think of stereotypes as pertaining to minority groups like women and racial minorities, but there are all kinds of other stereotypes, including political stereotypes.

Media Promoted Stereotypes: The USA

Without doubt, many media outlets are highly politically polarized, explicitly endorsing or promoting a particular political viewpoint. In the United States, FOX News and CNN are often seen as the two ends of a political pendulum, with FOX News as the conservative, right-wing outlet and CNN as the liberal, left-wing outlet. Of course, this view is itself a stereotype.

Media Promoted Stereotypes: The UK

In the UK the BBC News is considered Liberal, whereas Sky News is considered more Conservative.......Unlike the USA, British Newspapers are much polarized between the Sun Newspaper, and The Telegraph are viewed as Conservative publications, The Guardian and Independent are considered to endorse liberal views.

Political Party Stereotypes

The U.K like the USA is run on a two-party system, which means the vast majority of the political world is controlled by the Liberal (Labour Party) and (Tory Party).

Conservative Stereotypes of Liberals:

According to the media (and particularly conservative media), the Democratic Party (USA) and the Labour Party (UK) are supported by a bunch of "bleeding heart liberals" or "tree huggers" - people who are controlled by their emotions and being obsessively politically correct, especially when talking about minority groups.

Liberal Stereotypes of Conservatives:

On the other hand, liberal media outlets perpetuate a variety of stereotypes about the Tory and Republican Party. Republicans and are viewed as crazy cowboys who love guns, or as zealously religious aggressive and warmongering, while Tories are considered snobbish, elitist warmongers.

Specific Party Stereotypes

There are many stereotypes outside the traditional Republican/Democrat divide. Members of the Social Democrats (UK) Green Party, for example, are stereotyped in specific ways. Political movements like Occupy Wall Street and the Tea Party and the British National Party have associated stereotypes as well.

The Realities of Political Stereotypes

Political landscapes in other countries outside the UK and USA come with their own set of specific stereotypes. Sometimes we laugh at stereotypes of people on the "other side" of the political spectrum, and usually it's all in good fun. These stereotypes can be harmful though, so it's important to recognize that all they are is stereotypes. In reality, Labourite's, Democrats and Conservative and Republicans come in all different shapes, sizes, and belief systems. Stereotypes can get in the way of productive political discussion.

SECTION THREE:

LOOKISM:

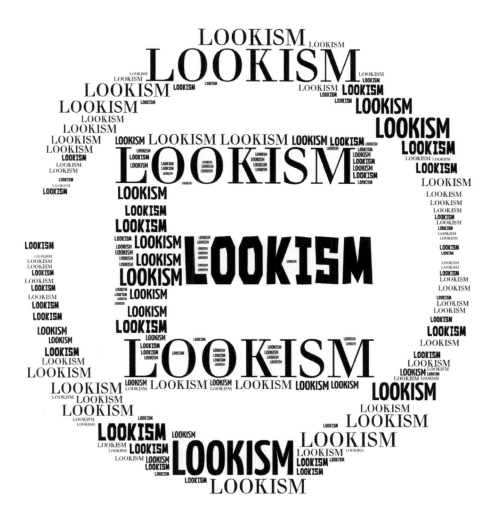

WHO YA LOOKING AT?

LOOKISM

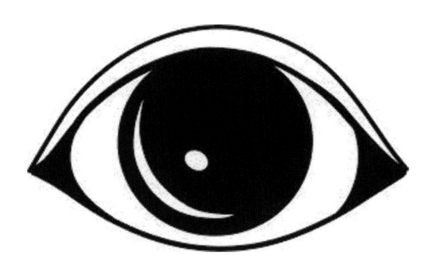

Aim	Identify how appearances affect bias
Group Size	20 Participants.
Materials	Flipchart and markers
Duration	1.2 Hours

Instructions:

1. Divide the group into smaller groups of five (5) people.

2. Divide the class into small groups - about 4 learners to a group and issue each group a flipchart and markers.

3. Each group will make two flipcharts. One will be titled "How prejudices and bias focus on the physical characteristics of people" and the other will be titled "How prejudices and bias focus on the dress and makes up of people".

4. Under each title they will list how people are hindered for not meeting a group's or organizational standards (norms).

5. Coach the groups as they work their way through the exercise.

6. These are some of the items that could be listed:

Physical Characteristics

a.   Too short

b.   Overweight

c.   Too light or too dark

d.   Too young or too old

Dress and Makes Up

1. Dresses out of fashion

2. Body piercing

3. Hair length

4. Informal dress

5. Impression of informality

6. Expression of cultural, ethnic, religious, generational, or personal standard. After the small groups have worked on the activity for about 25 minutes, bring the groups together and have each group present their findings.

Issues to discuss

1. Discuss what is fair and legitimate to ask of people when it comes to workplace norms about physical characteristics and appearances:

2. Ability to do the job.

3. Loss of customers and money due to how an organization's personnel look. Safety requirements.

4. Loss of good personnel because of bias about appearance.

LOOKISM

Lookism: Identify how appearances affect bias.

This exercise should enable participants to understand why automatic judgments of others are based on physical appearance and how these judgement influence people respond to each other.

Lookism is a term used to refer to the positive stereotypes, prejudice, and preferential treatment given to physically attractive people, or more generally to people whose appearance matches cultural preferences.

The term "Lookism" was first coined in the 1970s within the fat acceptance movement. It was used in The Washington Post Magazine in 1978, which asserted that the term was coined by "fat people" who created the word to refer to "discrimination based on looks." The word appears in several major English language dictionaries, and has received scholarly attention both from a cultural and an economics perspective.

In the former context, lookism relates to preconceived notions of beauty and cultural stereotyping based on appearance as well as gender roles and expectations. Important economic considerations include the question of income gaps based on looks, as well as increased or decreased productivity from workers considered beautiful or ugly by their co-workers.

In a culture in which the physical body is held in such high esteem and given such power, body fascism then not only deems those who don't or can't conform to be sexually less desirable, but in extreme sometimes dubbed lookism also deems a person completely worthless as a person, based solely on his exterior. In this sense it is not unlike racism or sexism, or homophobia itself."

THE COMMON BODY

Aim	To discuss prejudices to naturally occurring physical differences that occur in humans.
Group Size	10-40 participants
Material	The template, markers and free space in which the participants can speak in small groups.
Duration	20 Minutes

Description

Ask participants to tell the group about one unique thing about their body, not caused from an injury or activity—that is something that 'naturally' occurred. They can show the group as well, if they feel comfortable.

At first, people may not think they have an answer. You can offer examples, such as being double jointed or being able to move in uncommon ways, having an unusual patch of skin or birth mark**, having extra or missing parts.

As you go around, you might notice that some people who thought they had a unique part of their body really share that trait with another person in the room. People might also gradually remember other things about their body. If someone can't think of something, go on and come back to them later. After the exercise, ask about initial reactions.

Did the exercise make them think differently about themselves or the group, or about how normal the human body is?

Possible directions of conversation:

You might ask how many would have their bodies changed if there was surgery to do it. Ask them to think of examples when people have altered their bodies to fit into the norms of our culture. What are their reactions to that?

1. You might ask them to consider how they think of people more extremely different than them, people with diseases or syndromes or disabilities. Can they imagine these people also being content with their bodies and not wanting to change them?

2. There are studies of blind people who, with surgery, were given sight as adults. Many of them had a hard time adjusting to their new sense. Some did not like the lack of privacy that sight created when they came to realize people were watching them all the time. Some had a hard time learning how to use their eyes and preferred to keep their eyes closed. Some even wanted to return to blindness.

3. If you were told you were missing a sixth sense most other humans had, would you want it 'restored'? If you did, it would 'flood' into your brain, constantly, like your other senses, but more powerfully because it was new and unusual.

4. There are people born who are not clearly male or female. Their bodies differ from the norm of what it means to be female or male. They are known as intersex children. Often they are

surgically changed soon after birth, so that they look more 'normal', though there is nothing 'wrong' with them. They do not get to be a part of the decision.

Possible Question for Participants

1. Do you think intersex children should be surgically altered?

2. Would you have your child altered if they were intersex?

3. What if they were physically different in some other way that was not harmful to them but was outside of the norm?

4. If scientists discovered that they could determine a child's sexuality (gay straight or bi) at birth and could alter it, would you have your child changed if it was not what you were expected or wanted?

5. Additional time may be needed for discussion. **Note: if someone points or talks of an oval scar on their shoulder as a birthmark, it is most likely a TB shot given to them at birth.

6. You might bring this up and discuss, non-judgmentally, what it means to have had our bodies changed at birth, and to not know about marks on our own bodies.

Facilitator Notes

The Intersexed Condition

1Broadly speaking, intersexuality constitutes a range of medical conditions in which an individual's anatomy mixes key masculine anatomy with key feminine anatomy. There are a several conditions in which the child's genetic make-up is not clearly male (XY) or female (XX).

Klinefelter's Syndrome

Instead of the typical, XX or XY chromosome pattern, the child is born with an XXY pattern. The condition is not hereditary and seems to develop in the fetus. The extra X chromosome results in feminizing effects on the body. They are typically seen as boys and are raised as boys. The condition is often not diagnosed until puberty, when expected secondary sexual characteristics don't develop. These individuals are sterile, have enlarged breasts, small testicles & penis, tall in stature with long legs and short trunk, and are often learning disabled. Testosterone therapy seems to help with many of the results of Klinefelter's, with the exception of sterility.

Turner's Syndrome (XO)

These are females that are born without a second X chromosome. 1 in 2,000-2,500 births. Not hereditary. They tend to be short in stature (average height of 4'8" if not treated with growth hormones). They tend to have ovarian failure which results in a lack of development of secondary sex characteristics. 99% are infertile. Hormone replacement therapy can help.

Androgen Insensitivity Syndrome

Occurs in about 1 in 13,000 births. These individuals have a male genetic make-up (XY chromosomes). Testes develop during gestation, while the fetus is developing. These testes produce Mullerian Inhibiting Hormone (MIH) which prevents the development of a uterus, fallopian tubes, and cervix. The testes also produce testosterone. However, because cells fail to respond to testosterone, the genitals form in the female, rather than the male, pattern. Newborn infants may have the genitals of a normal female appearance. There is a short vagina with no cervix. Occasionally, the vagina is nearly absent. At puberty, the estrogen produced by the testes produces breast growth. She does not menstruate and is not fertile. AIS is a genetic defect located on the X chromosome, it runs in families. The mother of an AIS individual is a carrier, and her XY children have a 50% chance of having AIS. Her XX children have a 50% chance of carrying the AIS gene. AIS women tend to have a feminine gender identity.

Congenital Adrenal Hyperplasia

Occurs in both males and females. Occurs in about 1 in 13,000 births. In females (with an XX chromosome make-up), hypersecretions of steroid hormone from the adrenal gland causes masculinization of the external genitalia of the female fetus. Affected infants can have mixed genitalia. Internal female organs are intact. Many of these children receive "corrective" surgery during infancy. If the child is raised as male, following any "adjusting" surgery and given male hormones at puberty, the individual develops as a "normal" but sterile male with XX chromosomes. On the other hand, if the infant is surgically corrected to female and given female hormones, there is a 50/50 chance of transsexualism. So – this is more evidence that gender identity may be greatly influenced by hormones during development in the womb (rather than by chromosomal make-up).

Corrective Surgery

This "correction" is the source of much unhappiness – most advocates for intersexed individuals promote not performing any corrective surgeries on children and raising them as either as a boy or girl following consultation with medical professionals who are familiar with intersexed conditions. But the parents should watch for signs of gender expression in the child, not attempt to suppress these expressions if they don't fit with the gender they are being raised as, and when the adolescent is old enough to understand their condition, they should be informed and given the choice whether or not to proceed with surgery if an incongruity between physical sex and gender identity exists.

WHOM TO LEAVE BEHIND

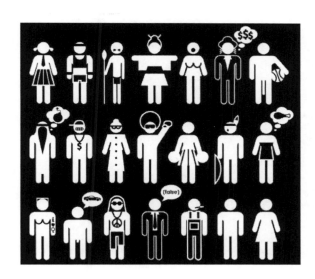

Aim	To assess our perspectives on diversity, tolerance and acceptance.
Group Size	10-12
Materials	The template, markers and free space in which the participants can speak in small groups.
Duration	60 Minutes

Instructions:

1. The twelve persons listed below have been selected as passengers on a space ship for a flight to another planet because tomorrow the planet Earth is doomed for destruction.

2. Due to changes in space limitations, it has now been determined that only eight persons may go. Any eight qualify.

3. Your task is to select the Eight (8) passengers who will make the trip.

4. On your own, take approximately 5 minutes and rank order of the passengers from one to twelve based on those who you feel are most deserving to make the trip with one being most deserving and twelve being least deserving.

5. Next, the entire group will come together and decides as a group the eight (8) passengers who will make the trip. PLEASE

6. NOTE: When you make your decision as a group EVERYONE must agree on the final eight passengers and come to a consensus. You are NOT allowed to vote or take a 'majority rules' decision.

Original passenger list:

1. An accountant with a substance abuse problem

2. A militant African-American medical student

3. A 33 year old female native American manager who does not speak English

4. The accountant's pregnant wife

5. A famous novelist with a physical disability

6. A 21-year old, female, Muslim international student

7. A Hispanic clergyman who is against homosexuality

8. A female move star who was recently the victim of a sexual assault

9. A racist armed police officer who has been accused of using excessive force

10. A homosexual male, professional athlete

11. An Asian, orphaned 12-year old boy

BROWN EYES

Aim	To understand the relationship between genes and stereotypes
Group Size	Any size
Materials	People with Brown Eyes
Duration	10 minutes

Instruction:

1. The facilitator tells participants that according to the latest discoveries of science the genes of intelligence are tied to the colour of the eye.

2. As a consequence the participants have to change places, so all those with brown eyes should sit at the front of the class. The others are to sit at the back.

3. After the participants change places, ask them to write down what they think about the reasons for this exercise.

4. After reading their answers aloud the discussion should move on to the bases of prejudices.

5. Why do we categorise people into, for example, white-black, European-African, Christian-Jew, thin-fat,boy-girl?

6. What are the reasons for such categorisation?

7. What consequences could they have?

8. Then ask them for examples about having been discriminated against, or being the one who did the discrimination.

Evaluation:

9. Ask them how they felt during the exercise and what they have learned from it.

Going further:

10. The facilitator can use the exercise to introduce discussion about ideologies such as National Socialism or racism. Depending on the development of the debate, it is possible to explain racism and point out that there is no difference between people, there is only one race within humanity: Homo Sapiens. We are all alike notwithstanding the colour of our skin or that of our eyes.

Please note:

1. In classes where all the participants have brown eyes, you can change the characteristic which divides them for the exercise.

2. Examples can be: height (tall/small); hair (curly/straight); etc.

Using space here

Ask your participants to pick two or three young people at random from *Space*: which ones do they think are 'at the front of the class'? / 'at the back of the class'?

SEGREGATING
THE X'S FROM THE O'S

Aim	To show how even mild affiliative preferences at the individual level can lead to surprisingly strong patterns of segregation at the group level, without any intentional desire or plan for segregation
Group Size	10-12 Participants
Material	1. An overhead projector
	2. An overhead transparency slide showing a check board grid with the squares numbered 1-64)
	3. 25 small gasket rings that create "O's" when placed on a square.
	4. 30 tile spacers that create "X's" when placed on a square.
	5. Other objects, such as pennies and paperclips, can also be used.

Duration   20 Mins

Preparation

Before class begins, arrange 30 "X's" (the majority) and 25 "O's" (the minority) in a random pattern on the check board so that 55 squares are covered and the remaining 9 squares are free.

Activity

Turn on the projector and tell participants to imagine that the check board is a community of 55 families and 9 unoccupied houses.

Explain that for purposes of the demonstration, a square's "neighbourhood" consists of the squares adjacent to it:
1. 8 squares for interior houses,
2. 5 squares for houses on the edge,
3. 3 squares for houses in a corner position).

Then tell participants that:

1. Each "O" wants to live in a neighbourhood with at least two other minority neighbours (a very modest preference).

2. Each "X" wants to live in a neighbourhood where most of its neighbours are majority members (again, a fairly modest preference -- not a desire to live in an all-majority neighbourhood).

3. In other words, if an "O" has fewer than 2 other "O's" next to it, the "O will be unhappy and want to move. Likewise, if the pieces surrounding an "X" are not mostly "X's," the "X" will want to move.

4. Then appoint a student to move unhappy pieces onto squares that will make them happy, and invite the rest of the class to call out moves (e.g., "Move the X on square 34 to square 17"), continuing until all pieces are happy.

5. In most cases, the end result will be a pattern of extreme segregation, even if participants have a desire for integration.

Variations

1. If time permits, you may wish to vary "X" and "O" preferences to see how the results change (e.g., by having "O's" prefer to be near 3 other "O's rather than 2).

2. You might also encourage participants to use pennies and dimes to experiment outside of class with different minority-majority ratios and decision rules, reporting any interesting findings to the class next time.

Notes

The lesson here is not to say that segregation is accidental -- merely that mild preferences at the individual level can lead to unanticipated or undesirable results at the societal level. More generally, the results show participants that their personal preferences matter and can play a role in creating social patterns that they may not prefer, such as self-segregated campus dining areas.

SHADISM AT WORK

		1	10			19	28	
		2	11			20	29	
		3	12			21	30	
		4	13			22	31	
		5	14			23	32	
		6	15			24	33	
		7	16			25	34	
		8	17			26	35	
		9	18			27	36	

Victoria and Janelle, both 16 years old, apply for casual jobs at a Caribbean fast food store. The store manager gets Janelle working on the register, and Victoria working in the kitchen.

Kwame and Janelle ask if they can swap jobs. The manager tells them that he prefers light skinned girls to work on the register because it 'looks better', and the people of a darker hue should work in the kitchen and stay out of sight as much as possible because a lot of white customers prefer to be served by light skinned people.

Victoria and Janelle think this is unfair, but the manager tells them if they don't like the work he has offered them they can find themselves another job.

What would you do if you were Kwame and Janelle

Options

A. Quit your job and find another one.

B. Put up with it. It's no big deal.

C. Get advice on what you can do.

Split the participants into 4 groups. Each group will be given this case to discuss and then present to the class.

Suggested Questions

What was wrong with is suggestion that men work at the back?

Did the manager make an unreasonable request?

Realistically, what could the manger have done to ensure that all his employees were being treated fairly?

Debriefing: (10 minutes)

Sum up the debriefing with a presentation of stereotypes, prejudices, discrimination and exclusion especially sexism.

THE BLACK BALLOON

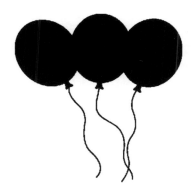

Author Unknown
The little black boy watched a man,
Blow up balloons one day
When each balloon was filled, the man
Let each one float away.
The little boy watched patiently,
And waved each one good-bye
As all the pretty bright balloons
Went drifting toward the sky.
He asked the man if black balloons
Would go up like the rest.
The man said, "Son, I'll blow one up,
And put it to the test."
And when the black balloon was filled,
They watched it rise and glide.
"It's not the colour, son," he said,
"But what you've got inside."

DISCUSSION

Young people often look to trusted adults to provide them guidance and clarity in life. This poem depicts a situation in which a young boy wondered if the colour of the balloon affected its ability to float away. This can be used to discuss how physical characteristics may or may not affect a person's potential in life. As you facilitate discussion be sure to talk about stereotyping and how it too may affect a person.

Questions

1. How different were the balloons in the story?
2. What did they all have in common?
3. Why do you think this man was filling balloons and then letting them float high into the sky?
4. What do you think made the boy ask about the black balloon?
5. Do the colours of people's skins determine who they are inside?
6. What do the colours of people's skins say about them?
7. Does the colour of your skin or a disability dictate your potential in life?
8. Will it help or hinder your from accomplishing your dreams and goals?
9. Why do people make predetermined judgments about others?
10. What should you do when people around you make judgments about another person?
11. How can you handle the situation?

SECTION FOUR:

LANGAUGE AND DIVERSITY

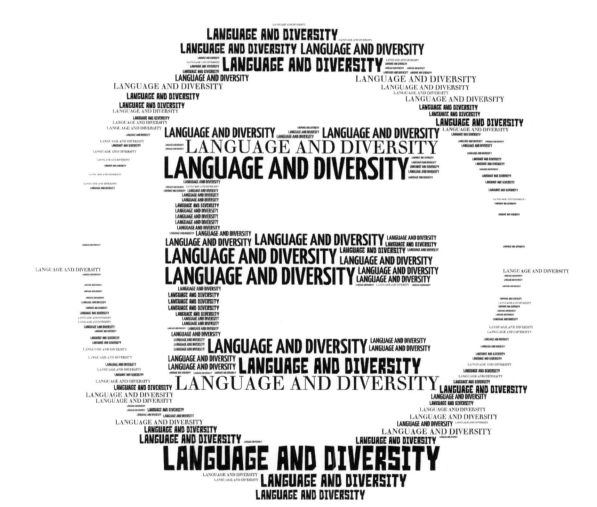

IT WAS A JOKE!

Aim	To understand the place of humour in relation to racism and prejudice
Group Size	Adults
Materials	Flipchart, Markers
Duration	45 minutes

Description

Participants were asked to bring three jokes. In groups of four to five, participants share the jokes and compare and contrast them in terms of the following criteria:

1.   Who was the joke aimed at?

2.   Who was the joke about?

3.   What is the joke about? Does it rely on history, myths or stereotypes?

4.   What is the purpose of the joke?

5.   What do all the jokes have in common?

Each group has 30 minutes before feeding back its conclusions to plenary.

The general discussion should include the hand-out Humour Can Be Used and the following questions if time allows:

1.   How are jokes used in oppressive thinking?

2.   How do they operate in terms of attitudes and opinions?

3.   Where do young people hear these jokes?

Check out how people feel listening and telling the jokes.

Posing the following question may help, listening to jokes, passive or active form of racism? What about us?

IT WAS A JOKE!

In today's multicultural and multi-religious societies, humour and comedy often become the focus of controversy over alleged racist or offensive content, as shown, for instance, by the intense debate of Sacha Baron Cohen's characters Ali G and Borat, and the Prophet Muhammad cartoons published in the Danish newspaper Jyllands-Posten.

What people find offensive and why is a question that does not have a simple answer. One person's joke is another person's rude comment. Some feel humour encourages stereotypes. Some feel it breaks them down. Let's look at some of the factors that account for some of these differences.

Conditioning By Society. We are programmed by our culture, family and other social influences to think that certain things are funny, and that other things are offensive, although it starts to be bad when the offensive humour begins to ruin relationships and eat away at a group's self-esteem.

Internalized Put Down. Some groups have lived with such a history of oppression that they've become conditioned to see negative put-downs in places where none was intended. Being offended becomes an automatic, knee-jerk reaction. You would think that ultra-sensitive reactions to humour would be easy to understand. But that's not the case…you haven't lived someone else's life. You see things only through your own filters.

The Psychic. Some people are offended because they always know WHY someone created a certain joke. They always know the motivation of the writer or speaker. Of course the truth is that they don't know the motivation. They are only guessing.

Your Intent. Get a good understanding on why you use humour. What is your motive behind a specific line? Is it that you really don't like the group you're poking fun at? When you're coming from a negative place, the humour is likely to be off target, offensive and divisive.

Notes

Sticks and Stones: To understand the value of language and its use. Participants will be able to identify and use appropriate language. Participants will be able to give examples of the consequences of the use of language.

What is or is not offensive language can often depend on the sensitivity of the listener, and although there are groups of words and phrases which will always be offensive, there is a debate to be had over words or phrases that may not be overtly offensive to some. In the workplace, it is the responsibility of the employer to ensure that their employees are not exposed to language that they may deem offensive or inappropriate. This means the employer must take active steps to ensure they have done everything possible to maintain an appropriate working environment.

Potential claims

It helps to first look at the potential claims that might arise where an employee is exposed to offensive language in the workplace. For a start, staff are protected from harassment and less favourable treatment on the grounds of race, sex, disability, sexual orientation, religious belief and age.

The problem for employers addressing this issue does not appear to lie in the extreme. A person using overtly racist language in the workplace is unlikely to be tolerated by either the employer or his colleagues and would most likely be dismissed fairly promptly. Problems tend to arise where language is said in 'jest', and where the individuals using the language did not understand or realise the potential offence that could be caused.

Indirect offence

There is another important category of complainant. Some individuals may observe the use of offensive language which, although not relevant or directed to them personally, they may still find offensive. That individual also has the right to bring this to their employer's attention, and if they are then subjected to detrimental treatment.

Circumstances can also arise where offensive or inappropriate language is used but may not be covered by discrimination legislation. This would then result in the employee having a grievance for bullying and harassment.

PARTNER TALK

Aim	To have participants appreciate the fact that their own communication styles although individual, are also influenced by culture.
Group Size	Any size; from 15 year old onwards
Material	Flipchart.
Duration	30 minutes

Description

1. Make enough copies of instruction slips. The slips should be cut so each participant receives one instruction: A, B, C, or D.

2. Give each participant one slip and instruct them not to share their rules with anyone.

3. Ask participants to pair off, preferably A's talking to B's and C's talking to D's. (If possible have them pair up with someone they don't know.)

4. Ask the pairs to talk to each other for two minutes, carefully following their own instructions. Their assignment is to find out two new things about their partner.

5. Reconvene the group.

Debrief: A

1. Ask participants if they found the exercise easy and have them describe their first reactions to the assignment.

2. List their responses on the flip chart.

3. Have one participant from each category (A, B, C, and D) read his or her rules aloud to the group. As the rules are read, list the following communication issues on the flip chart:

Debrief: B

A. Eye contact and the showing of emotion

B. Distance and gestures

C. Loudness and interruptions; initiating conversation and asking personal questions

D. Softness and no interruptions; not initiating conversation nor asking questions

4. Discuss what participants found most disrespectful, annoying, or embarrassing, and summarize by reminding them that culture often leads to different styles of communication.

5. Ask how the participants interpreted the behavior of their partners during the exercise. (For example, the person whose partner looked away felt that his partner couldn't be trusted, wasn't interested, or perhaps was bored.) It is important to recognize that there is a "mainstream" American communication style and that many different cultures bring with them their own rules and communication styles that are different.

Trainer's notes

The more a person understands differences in communication styles, the better communication can become. You may also suggest that matching styles can further positive communication across cultures.

Instruction slips for "partner-talk"

These instructions should be copied and cut into strips. Enough should be made so that each participant can be given one strip.

Group A Instructions

a) Avoid eye-contact when speaking to your partner.

b) Do not show any emotion or react to your partner when he or she is speaking.

Group B Instructions

a) Stand about six inches closer to your partner than you normally would.

b) Use gestures often when you are speaking.

Group C Instructions

a) Speak more loudly than you normally would and interrupt your partner fairly frequently.

b) Initiate conversation by asking a lot of questions (including personal ones).

Group D Instructions

a) Speak more softly than you normally would and don't interrupt your partner.

b) Silently count to six before responding and don't initiate conversation or ask questions.

THE BLACK BIRD

Aim	Using metaphors to enable participants to understand the importance of managing diversity.
Group Size	15 Participants
Materials	A copy of the Black board story
Duration	20 minutes

Preparation: Distribute the following story to participants

The Story

The second-grade school teacher posed a simple enough problem to the class. "There are four blackbirds sitting in a tree. You take a slingshot and shoot one of them. How many are left?" "Three," answered the first 7-year-old boy with certainty. "One subtracted from four leaves three." "Zero," answered the second 7-year-old boy with equal certainty. "If you shoot one bird, the others will fly away."

Discussion Questions

1. Pretend you were in the class. How would you have answered the teacher's question?

2. Why do you think the two 7-year-old participants answered the question the way they did?

3. Take a moment to think about what diversity means to you. Do you think it means the same thing to other people?

4. What's the correct answer?

5. Is there only one way to answer the question?

6. How do people's perspectives play a role in how they may answer the teacher's question?

7. Why do you suppose the first child answered, "Three," while the second child answered, "Zero"?

8. The author of this vignette illustrates the viewpoints of children who grew up in different environments. What is the lesson the author is trying to present?

Reflection

Do you think birds can be compared to human situations? Why or why not?

THE BLACK BIRD

1. **The Black Bird:** The aim of this exercise is to enable participants to understand how metaphors can be applied in the management of organizational diversity.

What is a Metaphor?

A metaphor is commonly known as an analogy between two objects or ideas, described by using another word. They also denote rhetorical figures of speech which have their effects on words through comparison, resemblance and association with many other things. Other figures of speech like hyperbole, simile and antithesis are all types of metaphors which also achieve their effects through the same way.

List of Common Metaphors

There are some common metaphors which are used almost by everyone in daily life and they go quite unnoticed. Find out which are those that you end up using many times from the ones mentioned in the list given below:

- A heart of stone
- Reality is an enemy
- He has the heart of a lion
- You are the sun in my sky
- Ideas are water
- You are the light in my life
- I'm dead tired

- You had better pull your socks up

- Drowning in the sea

- Words are false idols

- Jumping for joy

- Apple of my eye

The **Melting Pot**" Metaphor can be used to describe internal organizational cultures in which different ethnic metals are placed together over a hot fire to form an organizational cultural product that is stronger than any ethnic metal on its own, which suggests that the different organizational cultures should melt together as one, or assimilate instead of integrate.

Broth: This exercise should also enable participants to appreciate that organizational melting pot is actually like **Broth,** in which employees are considered ingredients but the stew is able to exist with many distinct flavours and textures, which still depends on the broth to hold the organization together. Each employee is considered an ingredient, that is able to maintain its distinct flavour and texture, but at the same time is influenced by the organizational Broth in which they float. Some ingredients are even softened by the broth, while still maintaining their distinct characteristics.

Colourful Salad In order for organizational diversity to be effective, participants should be encouraged to view employees in organizations as part of a **Colourful Salad,** in which racial groups are representative of different colourful vegetables, and fruits, that are combined together to enhance each other flavour and appearance without overshadowing or overpowering each other.

In managing diversity some organizational leaders prefer using a better metaphor such as a "**Pot of Stew**" where employees are seen as a variety of textures that are combined but all connected by the broth in which they work.

The organizational melting pot is actually like **Broth,** in which employees are considered ingredient, but the stew is able to exist with many distinct flavours and textures, but still depends on the broth to hold the organization.

Managing Diversity To address diversity issues, consider these questions:

What policies, practices, and ways of thinking and within our organizational culture have differential impact on different groups? It depends on the individual. We may share similar values, such as respect or need for recognition, but how we show those values through behaviour may be different for different groups or individuals. How do we know what different groups or individuals need?

Consequences of Ignoring Diversity

Ignoring diversity issues costs time, money, and efficiency. Some of the consequences can include unhealthy tensions; loss of productivity because of increased conflict; inability to attract and retain talented people of all kinds; complaints and legal actions; and inability to retain valuable employees, resulting in lost investments in recruitment and training.

SECTION FIVE:

DIVERSITY AND EQUALITY

:

DRAW YOUR OPINION

Aim   To introduce participants using their favourite ethnic food

Group Size   15-20

Materials

1. A sheet of A4 paper for each participants
2. Pens or pencils for delegates
3. A Flipchart or whiteboard
4. Blue tack or magnets

Timing

1. Explaining the Test: 5 minutes.
2. Activity: 5 minutes
3. Group Feedback: 10 minutes

Preparation

1. Delegates work individually in this task.
2. Ask them to sit with some space between them.
3. Distribute A4 sheets to delegates.
4. Ask the delegates to draw an object on their paper.

Examples include:
- **TV**
- **IPod**
- **Ladies shoes**

1. Allocate **3 minutes** for drawings.
2. Explain to delegates that you will not be answering any questions during this time and participants should work on their own without talking with others.

3. At the end of the **3 minutes**, collect the drawing and stick them on the flip chart or white board.

Discussion

Ask the delegates why no two drawings are identical even though the objects suggested are commonly known? Encourage a discussion based on how our values and interpretation of the world around us shape our views. Are the differences in the drawings important in shaping our opinion about others?

WORK PLACE IDENTITY

IDENTITY WHEEL EXERCISE

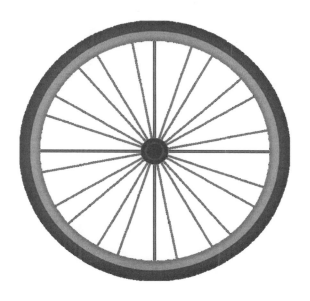

Aim   To establish if participants identities are targets for prejudice and discrimination or a privilege and advantage irrespective or employment or social status.

Group Size   15-30 Participants

Materials   Flipchart, Marker, Paper

Duration   20 minutes

Step One: Write down all of your (**Work Based**) identities your race, ethnicity, gender, organizational status, length of employment, pay grade, qualifications, and university attended etc.)

Step Two: Write down all of you (**Social Identities**) such as race, ethnicity, gender, marital status, sexuality etc.)

Step Three Categorize each **Work Based**) identity

Targeted (T): An identity that is the target of prejudice/discrimination

Advantaged (A): An identity that is privileged

Step Four: Categorize each **Social Identities**

Targeted (T): An identity that is the target of prejudice/discrimination

Advantaged (A): An identity that is privileged.

Step Three: Draw two circles two separate pieces of paper

Create pie charts on one piece of paper to show your **Social Identities** and   create another pie chart on a separate piece of paper to show your

Work Based that show you identities, in each section with the size of each pie piece relating to how aware you are of each identity on a daily basis.

Discussion Questions

1. Which identities were you more aware of?

2. Were the identities you are more aware of targeted or advantaged?

3. Why do you think that is?

4. Which identities do you take for granted and not think about often?

5. Were the identities you are less aware of targeted or advantaged?

6. Why do you think that is?

7. From this exercise, can you identify one or two identities in which you need to work on being more aware of?

8. What does this have to do with being an Ally?

THE EQUALITY DIALOGUE

Aim	Encourage to trainers to introduce topics like racism, sexism, classism, and heterosexism in the workplace and prepare them to handle the issues and exchanges that may result.
Group Size	15-30 Participants (Groups of four or five)
Materials	Flipchart, Marker, Paper
Duration	10 minutes

Description

1. Divide participants into groups of four or five.

2. Prepare enough space in the room for small groups to perform skits.

3. This activity will be most effective if you have already engaged in a discussion about the importance of dealing with issues of social justice in the classroom

Instructions:

Ask participants to share a story about a time when they participated in, or facilitated, a discussion on racism, sexism, classism, heterosexism, or another form of oppression that took an unexpected turn and caused conflict that was never resolved.

The situation may have ended in shouting or hard feelings or may have even deepened the tension being discussed.

Some questions to guide the discussion related to these stories:

1. What went wrong in the situation you shared?

2. How did the facilitator or educator or participants try to address the issue?

3. What about the tension?

4. How did the conversation end?

5.   How could the discussion have been more fruitful?

Ask each group to choose one story to role play for the rest of the class. Some people are less comfortable "performing" in front of the class, so encourage them and mention that everybody will have an opportunity to participate in a role play. Role plays should last no longer than 3 minutes.

After providing time for small groups to plan their role plays, ask for groups to volunteer to perform their role play for the class.

1. Following each role play, use or adapt the following questions to tease out the issues and strategies for addressing them:

2. What are the primary issues introduced by this situation?

3. What are the dangers of continuing a dialogue in response to the situation?

4. What are the educational opportunities introduced by the situation?

5. What are some strategies for managing the situation without immediately ending the conversation?

6. Following all of the role plays, process the activity by asking participants if they noticed any parallels in the stories.

THE EQUALITY DIALOGUE

1. To encourage to trainers to introduce topics like racism, sexism, classism, and heterosexism in the workplace and prepare them to handle the issues and exchanges that may result.

2. It is always important when activities call for participants to share their own stories and make themselves vulnerable to remind the group about active listening.

3. Consider starting the activity by sharing a story from your own experience to ease the tension.

4. You might also consider following this activity with one in which participants are encouraged to take turns facilitating conversations about issues of oppression for the other participants.

5. Consider using "plants" that are prepared to introduce difficult situations into the experience.

Backgrounds and Interests: You can learn a lot about other cultures by asking people about their backgrounds and interests. At staff meetings or luncheons, ask employees to take turns giving presentations about what life is like in another country, place, or ethnic group. They can share photos, along with ethnic food and recipes. This way, employees can learn about different customs, as well as lifestyle similarities and differences.

Travel Experiences: Asking employees about their travel experiences is a great way to discover differences and similarities with unfamiliar cultures. For example, people may tell you that they had a difficult time understanding the language, driving on the wrong side of the street, or trying new types of food.

Communication: Have employees observe each other's conversational styles. Even when speaking the same language, different cultures may use different words for describing the same thing. For instance, in some countries, "elevators" are called "lifts. "There are also dozens of expressions that are unique to and/or have different meanings in different cultures. It is also common for cultures to borrow phrases or expressions from other cultures. Your employees can have fun learning about similar expressions in other cultures, or, conversely, finding out phrases that mean the same thing, but are worded differently.

DIVERSITY!!

FAIRNESS OR BUSINESS

Aim	To explore whether diversity is a "Fairness" issue or a "Business" issue
Group Size	15 Participants
Materials	Flip chart
Duration	20 minutes

Procedure:

1. Point out to the participants that in many organizations, there is no complete agreement whether diversity is predominantly a fairness issue or a business issue. To explore this matter further, divide the group into smaller discussion groups. Ask them to select a reporter.

2. Assign half the groups to "Fairness" and the other half to "Business" and ask them to discuss both the pro's and con's of their side, jotting down key words as they come up. (You may want to start the groups off by offering them some challenging statements as listed in the Trainer's notes.) Allow 10 minutes.

3. Reconvene and ask the reporters to call out the points their group came up with. Enter on the flipchart the responses under two headings, "Fairness" and "Business". Comment on the responses, asking whether they are balanced or unbalanced, positive or negative, idealistic or realistic.

4. Lead a full group discussion, asking the group to provide its own overall answer to the question, "Is diversity a Fairness issue or a Business issue?

Debrief

1. Some of the points on one side or the other are clear-cut, while some others carry subtle shadings of meaning.

2. Explain that in workshops such as this, intuitively, the normal conclusion is that diversity is indeed both a fairness issue and a business issue.

3. Nevertheless, the value of this activity is that participants have an opportunity to explore the underlying issues and come to grips with different attitudes.

Discussion:

1. To help start the ball rolling in the discussion, you can use some possibly challenging statements such as the following:

2. Some people say that in their company, they haven't seen any diversity problems, so raising diversity issues is counterproductive.

3. Our company is already fair to all employees, why single out some for special attention?

4. Dealing with diversity is costly and time consuming, and does not add to the bottom line.

5. On the other hand, here are some positive comments which might be helpful:

6. It is important that both organizations and individuals create a better understanding among people from differing backgrounds.

7. Helping employees with special needs is the right thing to do.

8. A more diverse workforce increases creativity and innovation, and will increase recruitment possibilities and reduce turnover.

9. Today more than ever there is a need to establish the business case for Diversity and to ensure that the message is passed down throughout all levels of the organization.

Cultural Diversity in Organizations

Taylor Cox, Jr., Cox talks about three organization types that focus on the development of cultural diversity. The three types are: the **monolithic organization**, the **plural organization**, and the **multicultural organization**.

- In the **monolithic organization**, the amount of structural integration (the presence of persons from different cultural groups in a single organization) is minimal and white male privilege is very tangible. This type of organization may have women and marginalized members within the workforce, but not in positions of leadership and power.

- The **plural organization** has a more heterogeneous membership than the monolithic organization and takes steps to be more inclusive of persons from cultural backgrounds that differ from the dominant group. This type of organization seeks to empower those from a marginalized standpoint to encourage opportunities for promotion and positions of leadership.

- The **multicultural organization** not only contains many different cultural groups, but it values this diversity. It encourages healthy conflict as a source of avoiding groupthink

This is where establishing the business case for Diversity comes into play, it moves the emotional aspect out of focus and gives employees the 'real reason why it is so important for their organization to have a coherent Diversity strategy in place i.e. it is down to the effect on the bottom line business results as the company continually strives to establish its competitive advantage over and against the other companies operating in the same market space.

Diversity is not just a "Feel Good Issue" in fact it may be more of a correct statement to classify Diversity as "A Critical Business Issue" i.e. there is a compelling business case for diversity. Today's customers have a choice in purchasing products and services and; with the internet enable world that choice is becoming more and more global on a daily basis. In fact, companies who want to be the winners in their market space and particularly those who want to be big winners simply cannot afford to practice and conduct business with policies of exclusion in existence.

The companies who want to succeed are the ones who take Diversity beyond the Human Resources department and make it a part of the fabric of the everyday business transactions. These companies take Diversity to a level where they become role models to other companies in terms of inclusion as they welcome employees with different styles, different perspectives, different ideas, different passports, different accents and different skin colours into all levels of the business. These employees are welcomed and are used to make decisions, develop products, and engage with customers as a matter of course based upon their skill set.

The companies which innovate and reinvent themselves on a continuous basis are the companies which will retain their competitive advantage in the market place. Invention and innovation requires creativity and creativity requires true diversity.

Indeed the message that needs to be propagated throughout the organization is one that creativity is driven by true Diversity and, in turn creativity is the main driving force behind innovation and invention. It is this innovation and invention which enables companies to maintain their competitive advantage, this advantage drives profitability and this profitability continually establishes the business case for Diversity.

Recruiting, retaining, and promoting diverse employees are critical to a corporation's success in this evolving marketplace. These efforts must be carefully planned, nurtured, and measured to ensure success.

Corporate diversity initiatives must have total buy-in from top management, particularly from the CEO. Without support from the top, integration of diversity, inclusion and engagement strategies into corporate business plans and a company's culture are doomed to fail.

Corporations must now pay closer attention to the details of quality of life in the communities in which they are embedded as a basis for developing a renewal resource for highly talented associates, suppliers, and distribution partners.

It is important to note that diversity is all-inclusive. It does not refer solely to gender or race, but includes the characteristics that make each person individual. Diversity does not mean matching quotas, affirmative action or special privileges.

Implementing a diversity model is about creating a productive workplace where opportunities, treatment and practices are based on merit. It refers to a broad range of people, moving the issue beyond an "us versus them" viewpoint. And diversity is no longer seen as solely a legal or social issue, but as a business issue as well.

DIVERSITY LETTER GAME

Aim	To have participants define for themselves the meaning of diversity.
Group Size	15-30 Participants
Materials	Flipchart, Marker, Paper
Duration	10 minutes

Description

1. Show the participants the previously prepared flip chart and explain that the group's task will be to come up with what they feel makes up diversity (see Trainer's Notes).

2. Ask the participants to form pairs and think of as many words as possible for each letter on the chart in order to help clarify the term "diversity." Have them jot the words down on paper. Tell them that they have 3 minutes to complete this assignment.

3. After 3 minutes call "Stop," and then ask each pair to share the words that they chose for each letter.

4. Reconvene the group and have the participants call out their words. Write the responses on the flip chart and compare the responses of the various groups.

Debrief

Summarize by pointing out the variety of words that the participants used to define diversity.

Explain that diversity is a much broader term than race and gender, and that the challenge is to learn how diversity affects everyone, everywhere.

Trainer's notes

In preparation, print the letters spelling **"D I V E R S I T Y G A M E"** vertically on the flip chart, down the left side. Most of the letters lead easily to words describing diversity. Let the participants proceed on their own, but if they need help, you may jog their thinking by using some of the following examples:

D = disability, different styles

I = individuals, intelligence

V = varying, various, variety

E = education, economic status

R = race, religion

S = sexual orientation, social class, similarities

I = individuals, intelligence

T = thought processes, team efforts, traits

Y = youth, years

G = gender, geographical origins

A = age difference

M = multicultural

E = education, economic status

DIVERSITY LETTER GAME

The Diversity Letter Game: To have participants define for themselves the meaning of diversity.

What is Diversity?

Gender and race are generally the first two words that come to mind when asked to define diversity. Other **primary** definitions also include age, ethnicity and sexual orientation.

Secondary examples include religion, educational background, marital status, family status, income, first language, geographic location, work experience and communication style.

Secondary definitions of diversity are more variable in influence and less visible than **primary** definitions. However, they are all important human characteristics that affect one's values, opportunities and perception of self and others.

Today, diversity includes the perspectives brought to bear by intergenerational differences, international education and work experience, and a multicultural background. As organizations become increasingly global and/or expand domestic markets to include ethnic minorities, creating a diverse workplace has a strong impact on sales growth and innovation. In broad terms, diversity is any dimension that can be used to differentiate groups and people from one another. It means respect for and appreciation of differences in ethnicity, gender, age, national origin, disability, sexual orientation, education, and religion. But it's more than this. We all bring with us diverse perspectives, work experiences, life styles and cultures.

DIVERSITY CRAYONS

Author unknown

We could learn a lot from crayons:

Some are sharp,

Some are pretty,

Some are dull,

Some have weird names, and are all different colours,

But they all have to live in the same box.

DIVERSITY CRAYONS

Discussion

1. Appreciating diversity is valuing what makes us similar as well as different. This poem talks about learning to live together and appreciating the unique qualities of others.

2. Encourage participants to look around themselves and take note of all the things that make them who they are.

3. This poem is special because it can be adapted to discuss all areas such as gender, age, physical abilities, intelligence levels, racial/ethnic backgrounds, economic status, beliefs, family structures, places of residence, and so forth.

Questions

1. How are people similar to a box of crayons?

2. Have you met people who have distinct names or talk differently than you do?

3. How did you react when you first met them? How did they react to you?

4. Do the ways people look indicate their level of intelligence?

5. How can people with varying traditions, beliefs, and values learn to live together in the same community?

6. What would you expect to be the positive and negative about that type of situation?

7. What if everyone in the world was exactly the same? If they all looked the same, talked the same, shared the same views, practices, and traditions, what kind of world would it be?

THE DIVERSITY FISH BOWL

Aim: Fishbowl activities force participants to actively listen to the experiences of equality and diversity in the work place.

Group Size: Minimum of 12

Materials: None

Duration: 30 minutes

Instruction:

1. It is suggested that participants should restrict their discussions of equality and diversity to the following:
2. Race
3. Gender
4. Sexuality
5. Religion
6. Disability
7. Transgender

The discussion should focus on the participants' experiences in the following areas:

- Recruitment
- Selection
- Training
- Promotion
- Redundancy
- Pay
- Transfers

8. The following steps will set the ground rules, then initiate and process the dialogue for the student fishbowl activity:

9. One important ground rule must guide the participation of the observers:

10. During the course of the fishbowl, observers are not allowed to speak. Their job is to listen and learn from the fishbowl participants.

11. Mention that the observers will have an opportunity to discuss any issues that emerge in later processing dialogue.

12. If possible, assign one of the fishbowl participants the role of facilitator. It will be her or his responsibility to ask questions, facilitate the fishbowl discussion, and make sure everyone has an opportunity to talk.

13. If necessary, you can play the role of facilitator.

14. The topics to be discussed by the fishbowl can be developed to be relevant to your course or workshop.

15. For the most part, fishbowl participants should have an opportunity to take the conversation where they want - or need - it to go.

16. If it becomes necessary to push the conversation along, possible prompts include the following:

Instruction:

1. Make sure everybody in the fishbowl has an opportunity to talk.

2. Allow the fishbowl discussion to continue for at least 30 minutes.

3. You can allow it to continue longer if time permits.

4. When the fishbowl discussion winds down, divide the combination of your participants and the fishbowl participants into small groups of 6-10.

5. This will provide the observers an opportunity to ask for clarification on comments made during the fishbowl.

6. Instruct the observers that they are not to invalidate or question the participants' experiences or perspectives. They should use the small group discussions only to learn more from the fishbowl participants.

7. Allow at least 30 minutes for small group discussions.

8. After small group discussions, call everyone back together.

This will be the final processing discussion. A variety of questions can guide this conversation:

Reflection

To the observers:

Was it difficult to not respond to the fishbowl participants' comments during the fishbowl? Why?

To the fishbowl participants:

How did it feel to share your feelings about school, knowing that these teachers were listening closely?

To the fishbowl participants:

Do you usually have opportunities to share your perspectives on school and your education?

To the observers:

Did you hear anything from the fishbowl that surprised you?

Conclusion

To wrap up the entire exercise, pose a final question, giving everyone an opportunity to answer: What is one thing you have learned from this experience?

Facilitator Notes

1. A few simple strategies will help you facilitate this activity smoothly. First, remember that this activity is as much about reminding teachers that participants are their most important resources as it is about teaching.

2. As mentioned above, it is thus crucial that observers show maximum respect to the fishbowl participants by following the silence ground rule.

3. It may take some effort to enforce this ground rule, as many teachers are not fully ready to play the role of learner from people who may be their own participants. Consider writing something on the chalkboard or newsprint pad such as "We are all teachers. We are all learners."

4. Student fishbowl discussions are usually most successful when they are informal. Remember that the fishbowl participants have not had an opportunity to develop comfort with the participants of your class or workshop.

5. A noticeable level of tension is often evident in the room as teachers learn about their own possible deficiencies from participants, and participants try to respectfully critique the people who they have been taught to trust and respect.

6. A variety of strategies can be used to ease the tension, ranging from starting with a fun icebreaker to serving snacks.

CHOICES

Purpose

To experience how people make decisions when choosing those with whom they want to work

Time: 10 minutes

Equipment: none

Materials: none

Procedure

Ask the group to stand up and mill around as if at a reception or cocktail party.

Give the following instructions:

1. Each person's goal is to form a work group of 4–5 people. To do that, your task is to find people with similar histories, values, attitudes, work/family responsibilities, or even assumptions about others.

2. After you have met 1–2 participants who share things in common with you, your group will establish the criteria for others to join. For example, your group may find that you are all single parents who are concerned about child care.

3. Or perhaps you may have attended the same high school, enjoy the same hobby, or are active in specific social advocacy programs. As the criteria become fixed, only those who fit can join your group.

4. Reconvene to discuss the activity, asking questions such as:

5. How did you feel during this exercise?

6. Was it easy or difficult? Were there any surprises?

7. What factors entered into your decisions about whom to talk with?

8. What happened to those individuals you included?

9. What happened to you when you were included? Excluded?

Debrief

Close by pointing out that when people have a choice about those with whom they will work, the tendency may be to try to find people with more similarities than differences. In this way, we may exclude many others without realizing it.

DISMISSAL

A large organisation has had some problems recently and its equality policies have been inconsistently applied. Managers have been told to make sure that staff are 'kept up to the mark' for attendance and discipline and to take disciplinary action as necessary, including dismissing anyone who has reached their limit of oral and written warnings for misconduct. When a new manager arrives, there are four employees in their department who are in this position:

Terry is a 50 year old white British man. He has sometimes shouted at fellow workers and even at the previous manager, for which he was disciplined. He says his loss of temper is because of the pain he experiences from a long-term disability (a back condition).

Shireen is a 30 year old British Asian woman who has consistently ignored the dress code and been disciplined for this. She says that as a devout Muslim, she cannot wear her shirt tucked into her trousers because this would be immodest.

Sarah is a 24 year old openly gay white British woman who has missed several deadlines for finishing work. She has said she just could not fit everything in.

Richard is a 37 year old black British man. Before the new manager arrived, he had helped a colleague with a complaint that the colleague was being sexually harassed by a different manager. D has been disciplined for unrelated matters.

Question: *Looking at this just in terms of equality law (rather than any wider management issues), is it unlawful to dismiss any of these employees? If so, which?*

EXERCISE: ADVERTISEMENTS

A night club advertises its services on some flyers as follows:

1. Come to the best nightclub in town!
2. Over 21s only.
3. Ladies – you'll get two for one on drinks all night on Tuesdays.
4. Gents – no groups of 3 or more men admitted without accompanying ladies.
5. No hoodies or other head coverings allowed – just don't bother as you won't get in!
6. English must be spoken – we'll be checking!
7. Please note – our venue is unsuitable for pregnant women and disabled people.

Question: What is wrong with this advertisement?

Please list the wording which you think may unlawfully discriminate and say what is wrong with it.

ANSWER

Over 21s only: no problem with this at the moment. After 2011, the club will need to be able to justify this direct age discrimination.

Ladies – you'll get two for one on drinks all night on Tuesdays: this may well be unlawful direct discrimination because of sex – men are being treated worse just because they are men.

Gents – no groups of 3 or more men admitted without accompanying ladies: this is direct sex discrimination – groups of 3 women are allowed in but groups of 3 men are not, just because they are men.

No hoodies or other head coverings allowed: this discriminates against people of a number of religions who are required to wear a head covering, such as Muslims, observant Jews, Sikhs and Rastafarians. It would be unlawful unless it could be justified as a balanced way of achieving a worthwhile outcome (a proportionate means to a legitimate end).

English must be spoken: this is more likely to put people who cannot speak English at a disadvantage compared to people who speak English so is potentially indirect discrimination because of race – also some disabled people may be affected, for example, British Sign Language users or people with a severe speech impediment may not pass the declared check. It would be unlawful unless it could be justified as serving a legitimate aim (a proportionate means to a legitimate end). Altering this rule for disabled people who are affected by it may well in any event be a reasonable adjustment.

Our venue is unsuitable for pregnant women and disabled people: this blanket declaration could be unfavourable treatment of pregnant women or direct discrimination because of disability. It would not be pregnancy discrimination if the club could show that it is necessary to exclude pregnant women on ground of health or safety (which would bring them within a permitted exception), but they would need to provide evidence of this. For disability, it is not possible to make a blanket statement against disabled people as an entire group as there is such a range of impairments. So this wording is definitely unlawful. Because the club seeks to deny access to disabled people then it is likely that it would also be acting unlawfully as it is unlikely to be prepared to make reasonable adjustments.

SECTION SIX:

POWER PRIVILEGE AND STATUS

BOOT STRAPS

Aim	To analyze social privilege and multi-discrimination on equal opportunities
Group Size	15-30 Participants
Materials	Flipchart, Marker, enough space for participants to form a line side by side
Duration	80 minutes

Instructions

1. Ask the participants to form a line side by side and stay silent. The trainers call some categories and all the people identifying with it have to walk one step forward or one backward as indicated by the trainers, one step forward means that that category is a source of advantage in the society, one step backward means that it's a source of disadvantages (i.e. "If you are male one step forward")

2. If they reach a point when they cannot anymore hold the others hands they have to leave it. Create a list of statements involving different categories: age, studies, socioeconomic background, skin colour, ethnicity, religion, sexual orientation…

3. After reading a few ask the participants to stay on the place they are and put a "prize" a few meters from the participants. Tell the group it represent a goal they have (success…) and they will have to race for it… ready, steady…GO!!

4. Facilitate a discussion on what happened, (are we really starting from the same point? Not reaching the goal means not enough motivation? What is the effect of cumulative disadvantage?)

HIDDEN PRIVELEGE

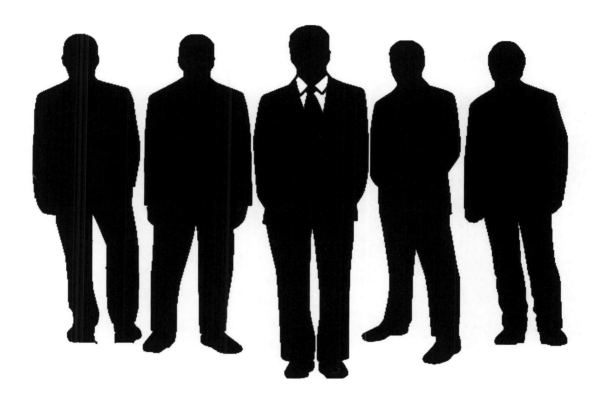

Aim   How to address work place dilemmas

Group   Any size

Materials   Flipchart, Hand-outs

Duration   Any

Scenario:

Johnny, one of your direct reports, just left your office. He brought an issue to you; now you have to determine what to do.

Here's the issue:

Amidst recent layoffs and downsizing, you promoted Sid, one of Johnny's peers, to a managerial role. Johnny believes he is just as qualified as Sid and he's frustrated that Sid got the job. Johnny believes you didn't even consider him.

Johnny told you he feels lucky to work at a company that hasn't been hit too hard in these tough economic times. He's worked for you for three years, and for the company, eight years. While there have been layoffs, the quality of Johnny's work has never been an issue or a concern. He's been a good worker, reliable and knowledgeable in his field.

Johnny is not claiming discrimination - he stated that clearly in your conversation. However, he said he thinks that there are some "systemic issues of privilege" going on and he wants you to address them. He left the meeting saying, "I expect you to do something with this information, or I will have to."

What are you going to do?

Option 1: You feel mildly perturbed. Sid has three more years' experience and has been a manager before. Johnny has never managed people. You needed someone who could step right into this role and do the job with little supervision. You will bring this issue to HR's attention and then loop back to Johnny to tell him you've done that, that you value his contributions and are glad he's part of the team.

Option 2: You have an "oh my gosh" moment. You realize that you picked Sid for some very good reasons and that you never considered Johnny - even though he has a good skill set. You tell Johnny that you are going to take a couple of days to think about what he said and will get back to him. In the meantime, you will sit down with your boss and also with HR to discuss your insights and the potential implications.

Option 3: You look Johnny squarely in the eye and tell him that you "blew it". You have so much on your plate, right now, that you are working on max-speed auto-pilot. You never considered other options. You promise when the next opportunity comes up, you'll consider Johnny.

Option 4: You realize that this issue could be larger than the Johnny/Sid issue. Even though Johnny did not say this was a case of discrimination, others might not believe that. Regardless, since he raised the issue of privilege, this has to be addressed. You know that these kinds of systemic issues can be subtle and often go unnoticed. This isn't something you've ever thought about. You are a good person; you work for a great company that has strong policies and practices. You decide to take this on - to figure out what the next steps are. - You let Johnny know your plan.

Hidden work place privileges should be understood in the current of political context by way of policies that have been introduced to ensure work place situations do not disadvantage one group over another......The usual methodology is by way of an equality policy

Job Descriptions and Person Specifications: Even when guidelines appear to be socially and politically sound, the identification of requirements remains subjective when it comes to draft a job description as judgement greatly depends on conclusions which are based on one's conceptualisations.

Application forms, multi-purpose may become a tool of discrimination as they can easily incorporate a discriminatory bias within their highly structured framework of recruitment and selection

Short listing: Research suggests that employers are prejudiced against certain groups of workers. Because of this prejudice, employers are said to sustain a cost when they hire someone from the group discriminated against. The effect of prejudice and bias is, therefore, difficult to control, and unfairness in short-listing is difficult to restrain. Other main initial steps in the recruitment and selection process offer no guarantee of fairness.

Selection Criteria: Suitability: There is a strong move towards competence based selection tests; this doesn't necessarily mean that success at these tests will mean job selection. In fact ability to learn on the job is given more weight than school qualifications.

Psychometric Testing: The use of cognitive and psychometric tests in their own right and at assessment centres still with respect to psychological testing, psychometric testing has been used to discriminate against ethnic minorities.

It is understood that the use of psychometric tests are inevitable, but there is increasing anecdotal evidence to suggest that African and African-Caribbean graduates are often reluctant to apply for jobs that use such tests. The perception is that such tests are culturally biased and are used as a means of further discriminating against ethnic minority graduates.

Interviewing: There is anecdotal evidence in which interviews have focused on the biographical aspect of the interview process because they are often surprised when they are faced with a highly qualified candidate that is Black graduate.

THE DASH FOR CASH

Aim	To demonstrate the relationship between wealth, power and economic inequality
Group Size	12 -25 users of words regarding colour

Materials	100 Coins, Mittens, Scoop
Duration	Open

Description

1. Explain to participants that in this activity they will distribute the wealth and power of the world among themselves. This wealth is represented by the 100 pennies.

2. There is only one rule: no participant may touch another member of the group at any time.

3. Arrange the room so that participants have a fairly large area to play the game.

4. Have participants stand or sit in a circle and **scatter the pennies** evenly in the middle of the circle.

5. **Withhold three** participants from this part of the activity.

6. Distribute **mittens** for some participants to wear but postpone discussion of reasons for this until debriefing.

Note: To emphasize that some start off with more than others, consider giving three or four participants five extra pennies to begin with as well as providing them with special scooping shovels.

1. At the order of GO, have participants (except the three withheld) gather as many pennies as possible without touching one another.

2. **Note:** Penalties for violations of this rule may be needed, such as removal from the game or payment to the person touched.

3. After all the pennies have been collected, have participants report their wealth to the class.

4. Record participants' names and number of pennies on a board or chart paper under three categories:

5. GREAT WEALTH AND POWER (those with six or more pennies—the smallest group);

6. SOME WEALTH AND POWER" (those with three to five pennies—the middle group); and

7. LITTLE WEALTH AND POWER (those with two or fewer pennies—the largest group).

2. Remind the group that these pennies represent their wealth and power in the world. The amount they possess will affect their capacity to satisfy their needs (e.g., basic education, adequate food and nutrition, good health care, adequate housing) and wants (e.g. higher education, cars, computers, toys, television and other luxury items).

3. Those participants with six or more pennies will have their basic "needs" and most of their "wants" met; those with three to five pennies will have their basic needs met, and those with two or fewer pennies will have difficulty surviving due to disease, lack of education, malnutrition, and inadequate shelter.

4. Tell participants that they may, if they wish, give pennies to others; however, they are not required to do so. Tell them that those who do share will be honoured as "DONORS," with their names placed on the board.

5. Allow a few minutes for participants to redistribute the pennies if they wish. Then ask for the names of those who gave away pennies and the amount each gave.

6. List them on the board or chart entitled "DONORS." Ask if anyone changed category as a result of giving or receiving pennies and record these shifts on the chart.

Debriefing the Activity

Note: Debriefing is an essential step in this process.

Draw on the following questions to promote a productive discussion.

Be sure to devote time to a discussion of changes needed and changes undertaken.

1. How did you feel about the way in which the pennies were acquired and distributed?

2. Were you treated fairly?

3. Did some people give pennies away?

4. Did you give away or receive pennies?

5. Why or why not? How did this feel?

6. What determined whether or not people gave away pennies?

7. Having one's name displayed?

8. Feeling guilty? Something else?

9. What aspects of this game represented how the world's wealth and power are distributed?

10. What about the three participants assigned to groups?

11. Were they fairly treated?

12. Is what happened to them similar to what happens to people around the globe?

13. What sorts of people? Is it just chance where we end up?

14. What about the participants with **mittens** (and **scooping shovels**)?

15. What kinds of people do the **mittens** (and **scooping shovels**) represent? What group did they end up in?

16. How did the members of the different groups feel about their situation?

17. Did the recommended plan for fair distribution reflect whether the group had more or fewer pennies?

18. After playing this game do you have a better understanding of the situation or attitude of poor people/nations?

19. Of the situation or attitude of wealthy people/nations?

20. Why were some people given more votes than others?

21. Was this an accurate

22. Representation of those with more or less power in the world?

23. Who are the "haves" and the "have nots" in the world today?

24. Which countries are the "haves" and the "have nots"?

25. Who are the "haves" and "have nots" in our country today?

26. In our state or community? Why?

27. Should the "haves" be concerned about the situation of the "have nots?"

28. For what reasons? Economic? Moral/religious? Political?

29. Why might the "haves" give money or resources to the "have nots"?

30. Is this a way to solve the problems of poverty?

31. What might the "have-nots" do to improve their situation?

32. What are some actions that "have-nots" have taken around the globe and at home to address the inequalities of wealth and power?

33. Do you think there should be a redistribution of wealth and power throughout the world?

34. Why or why not? If yes, how would you propose to accomplish this? What principles would guide your proposals for change?

35. Do you think there should be a redistribution of wealth and power in this country? Why or why not? If yes, how would you propose to accomplish this?

36. What principles would guide your proposals for change?

UNDERSTANDING PRIVILEGE

Aim   Participants share their experiences as participants, exploring different ways people are made to feel "included" in and "excluded" from the learning process.

Group Size   15 - 35 users of words regarding colour

Materials   Flipchart and markers

Duration   Open

ACTIVITY INSTRUCTIONS:

1. Participants are given a tally sheet.

2. Participants will listen to each of the privilege statements.

3. If the participant identifies with the statement and feels that it is true, they do nothing.

4. If the participant does not identify with the statement or feels like it is not true for their experience, they will draw one mark signifying that they do not identify with that particular privilege.

PRIVILEGE STATEMENTS:

1. The leader of my country is also a person of my racial group. (RACE)

2. When going shopping, I can easily find clothes that fit my size and shape. (SIZE)

3. In public, I can kiss and hold hands with the person I am dating without fear of name calling or violence. (SEXUALITY)

4. When I go shopping, I can be fairly certain that sales or security people will not follow me. (RACE/APPEARANCE)

5. Most of the religious and cultural holidays celebrated by my family are recognized with days off from work or school. (RELIGION/CULTURE)

6. When someone is trying to describe me, they do not mention my race. (RACE)

7. When I am angry or emotional, people do not dismiss my opinions as symptoms of "that time of the month." (GENDER)

8. When expressing my opinion, I am not automatically assumed to be a spokesperson of my race. (RACE)

9. I can easily buy greeting cards that represent my relationship with my significant other. (SEXUALITY)

10. I can easily find hair products and people who know how to style my hair. (RACE)

11. In my family, it is seen as normal to obtain a college degree. (CLASS)

12. If I am going out to dinner with friends, I do not worry if the building will be accessible to me. (ABILITY)

13. I can be certain that when I attend an event there will be people of my race there. (RACE)

14. People do not make assumptions about my work ethic or intelligence based upon the size of my body. (SIZE)

15. When I strongly state my opinion, people see it as assertive rather than aggressive. (RACE/GENDER)

16. When I am with others of my race, people do not think that we are segregating ourselves.(RACE)

17. I can feel comfortable speaking about my culture without feeling that I'll be judged. (RACE/ETHNICITY)

18. I can usually afford (without much hardship) to do the things that my friends want to do for entertainment. (CLASS)

19. When filling out forms for school or work, I easily identify with the box that I have to check. (GENDER/RACE)

20. I can choose the style of dress that I feel comfortable in and most reflects my identity, and I know that I will not be stared at in public. GENDER/APPEARANCE)

21. If pulled over by a police officer, I can be sure that I have not been singled out because of my race. (RACE)

22. My professionalism is never questioned because of my age. (AGE)

23. I do not worry about walking alone at night. (GENDER)

24. People do not make assumptions about my intelligence based upon my style of speech. (RACE)

25. When attending class or other events, I do not have to worry about having an interpreter present to understand or to participate. (ABILITY/LANGUAGE)

26. I can book an airline flight, go to a movie, ride in a car and not worry about whether there will be a seat that can accommodate me. (SIZE/ABILITY)

27. People assume I was admitted to school or hired based upon my credentials, rather than my race or gender. (RACE/GENDER)

28. As a child, I could use the "flesh-colored" crayons to color my family and have it match our skin color. (RACE)

PROCESS QUESTIONS:

1. How did you feel doing this activity?

2. How was it to consider the number of tally marks you had on your paper?

3. How was it to notice the tally marks of others around while you were or were not making marks on your page?

4. What does it feel like to have or not to have certain privileges?

5. What is privilege? How would you define it?

Notes:

DEFINITION OF PRIVILEGE:

1. Privilege is an invisible package of unearned assets which I can count on cashing in on each day, but about which I was "meant" to remain oblivious. In fact, privilege is an invisible weightless backpack of special provisions, assurances, tools, maps, guides, codebooks, passports, visas, clothes, compass, emergency gear and blank checks guide your proposals for change?

2. Privilege is a key element in perpetuating oppressive systems. According to Webster's Dictionary, privilege is "a right, favor, or immunity, granted to one individual or group and withheld from another." By having an oppressor exercising privilege that favors one over the other and not questioning the system or being invested in dismantling it, then oppressive systems are maintained.

3. We are going to spend some time examining the privileges that we hold. Sometimes we only look at areas that we are oppressed – wanting to focus on others' power and responsibility to change the dynamic. However, it is not always "someone else's" problem. So we want to take a little closer look at the privileges we may or may not hold

Facilitator Notes on Privileges

Those attitudes, behaviours, and pervasive and systemic social arrangements by which members of one group are exploited and subordinated while members of another group are granted privileges

Two types of privileges:

1. Unearned entitlements-privileges we should all possess
2. Conferred dominance-one person/group power over another

White privilege:

1. White privilege is the "system of benefits, advantages, and opportunities experienced by white persons" given purely based on race/skin colour (Donnelly, Cook, Van Ausdale & Foley, 2005, p. 6). Social Class Privilege:

2. Typically, social class is associated with income, occupation, and education; thus, power, wealth, social networking attribute to the distinction of the different classes.

3. 3 components: "a social class of origin, a current felt social class and an attributed social class" (Barrett, 2007, n.p.).

Gender Privilege:

1. Attributed to by invisibility
2. Research shows that class differentiation may serve as a proponent of gender privilege.
3. Women are economically and socially disadvantaged throughout society (Evans, et. al, 2010)

Heterosexual Privilege:

1. Most invisible privilege
2. Heterosexuality is viewed as normal and other sexual orientations are viewed as wrong or deviant.

Ability Privilege:

1. People with disabilities are anything but equal to the normalcy of society, whether by thought or action on the "designated" level prescribed, tends to concentrate on the mental and physical attributes of an individual.

2. Society also continues to utilize pity and discount the talents and skills of those with a disability.

Christian Privilege:

1. Specific areas have dominant religious traditions and others tend to be discounted or viewed as a lesser amongst the society.

2. Those with Christian privilege have a responsibility to reflect on their privilege and power and create more equitable religious identification patterns" (Evans et al, 2010, p. 243).

3. Christians are generally accepted and used in public arena and education, while other religious groups are not afforded the same experience.

References

http://studentdevelopmenttheory.wordpress.com/complexities-of-social-identity-development/

Abes, E. S., Jones, S. R., & McEwen, M. K. (2007). Reconceptualizing the Model of Multiple Dimensions of Identity: The Role of Meaning-Making Capacity in the Construction of Multiple Identities. Journal of College Student Development, 48(1), 1-22.

Barrett, W. (2007, April 225). Talking about social class on campus. NASPA's Net Results. Retrieved May 25, 2009, from http://wbarratt.indstate.edu/documents/talking_about_social_class.htm.

Bohmer, S., & Briggs, J.L. (1991). Teaching privileged participants about gender, race and class oppression. Teaching Sociology, 19, 154-163.
Donnelly, D.A., Cook K.J., Van Ausdale, D., & Foley, L. (2005). White privilege, color blindness, and services to battered women. Violence Against Women. 11(1), 6-37.

Evans, N. J., Forney, D. S., Guido, F. M., Patton, L. D., & Renn, K. A. (2010). Student development in college: Theory, research, and practice (2 ed.). San Francisco: Jossey-Bass.

Frye, M. (2003). Oppression. In M.S. Kimmel & A. L. Ferber (Eds.), Privilege: A reader (pp.13-20). Cambridge, MA: Westview Press.

Jones, S. R., & McEwen, M. K. (2000). A conceptual model of multiple dimensions of identity. Journal of College Student Development, 41(4), 405-414.

Young, I.M. (2000). Five faces of oppression. In M. Adams, W.J. Blumenfield, R. Castaeda, H.W. Hackman, M.L. Peters & X. Zuniga (Eds.), Reading for diversity and social justice: An anthology on racism, anti-Semitism, sexism, heterosexism, ableism, and classism (pp.35-49), New York: Routledge.

Zack, N. (1995). Life after race. In N. Zack (Ed.), American mixed race: The culture of microdiversity (pp. 297-307). Lanham, MD: Rowman & Littlefield.

NO POWER

Aim   To explore the experience of feeling powerless, to express it visually and to try out alternatives and see their effect.

Group Size   Variable, in groups of three

Materials   None

Step by step description:

1. Ask participants to think individually of one incident in which they felt powerless and unable to do anything about it. It could be a situation that they tried but failed to change, or one in which they would have liked to achieve a different outcome. (**5 minutes**)

2. In groups of three, each person in turn silently sculpts the rest of the group into three tableaux that depict the beginning, the middle and the end of the situation. It is necessary to tell people who they are only if they are confused about what they are representing in the tableau. (**10 minutes**)

3. When all the groups have produced the set of tableaux for each of their members, they choose one of the stories to work on. Run the sequence of tableaux again for the chosen story, this time incorporating one spoken thought for each of the characters – that is, one thought in each tableau. The thoughts should be spoken in a predetermined order.

4. Working on the same story, extend the tableaux and thoughts into three short scenes – no more than a minute for each one. Each person turns their thought into a sentence, combining it with some appropriate physical action. (**5 minutes**)

5. Come back to the whole group and see the work from each subgroup. Choose one of the subgroups to use in a demonstration. Take a tableau

which has an easily identifiable oppressor, and an oppressed person with whom we can feel sympathy.

6. Ask the rest of the participants to suggest how the powerless person might act to alter the situation. Try out these suggestions, with the participant who has the new idea going into the piece and playing the person whose actions they want to change.

7. Continue this process with each of the stories, either as one group or with two of the groups joining together and serving as an audience for each other. **(15 minutes)**

Reflection and Evaluation:

1. What is the effect of different actions on the outcome? How does the exercise relate to the lives of participants? What can they take away with them from this work? **(5 minutes)**

Comments:

1. It is important that the group works on creative alternatives to the powerless response, rather than merely criticising it.

2. A group will often be able to see solutions that the individual does not see.

NO POWER

To explore the experience of feeling powerless, to express it visually and to try out alternatives and see their effect.

Powerless

For the person that feels powerless, it comes from a perspective that one does not have an effect on their environment. However, this doesn't' necessarily relate to all situations. While one person may feel empowered in one area of life, when it comes to another area they may feel powerless.

Or it could be a general feeling of being powerless and this will mean that it will affect ones behaviour in a variety of ways.

The Inner Experience

Internally this will lead to different feelings, thoughts, emotions and sensations. Feeling powerless is the obvious feeling and then one can also feel: depressed, hopeless, frustrated and angry. Anger is often the result of one feeling that they have been compromised. And if one feels powerless then compromise will be a common experience; so it is the not much of a surprise if this person feels deep anger.

The Outer experience

If one feels powerless within it may seem that they will appear that way without. But this does not always happen. This can lead one to wanting to control others and to go to the other extreme of being in complete control of their environment. For some it will lead to these internal feelings being clearly visible to the outside world. This could be in form of one always appearing as the victim, unfortunate and as a slave to circumstances.

Dysfunctional examples of this are dictators, tyrants and extremely controlling people; these are people who, out of their own sense of powerlessness, need to control everyone and everything as a way to cover up what they feel within.

Regulation

What control does is allow for one to regulate these inner aspects. And yet if one feels these things within, it will not matter what goes on outside. No matter how much one consumes, in terms of possessions or people, it will never last or be enough power.

Perception

So if we were to round up two groups of adults, one group who feel empowered and another group that feel disempowered; on the surface there is probably not a lot of difference. What will be different are the perceptions that they have. Physically they are all adults and when it comes to their mental and emotional sides there is a difference. One group perceives the world through the eyes of an adult and the other through the eyes of child

Regression

When the past has not been processed or dealt with, it will lead to one regressing to the past. And to one perceiving the present based on associations that were formed when one was very young. At these moments it becomes extremely difficult for one to be present and to see that they do have an effect.

Evaluation and Reflection

1. Conclude by pointing out that regardless of our backgrounds, those things that are very important to us are often similar for all of us.

2. So, if you found yourself on a deserted island with someone you consider to be very different from you, and you think you couldn't possibly have anything to talk about, think about your pipe cleaners and you will have plenty to talk about.

3. The same principle could apply to almost any situation in which you are interacting with someone who has a background different from yours.

THE JELLY BEAN TEST

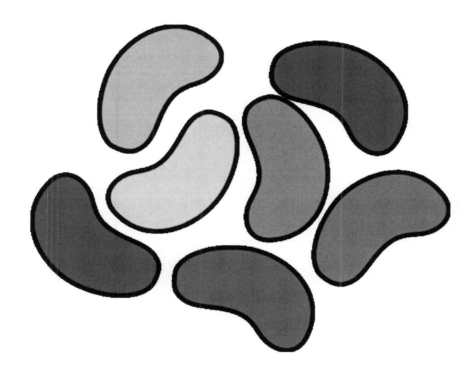

Aim	To enable participants to discover why the colour of the chosen Jelly Bean may be linked to personality.
Group	Any size
Material	Jelly Beans, Wine Gums or Smarties

Duration   Any

Instructions:

1. With a large selection of each colour of jelly bean, ask each person to take one, considering the colour of the jelly bean. (M&M's may be used as well, but some colours may have to be eliminated.)

2. Tell the group to hold the jelly bean and not eat it.

3. Ask for a show of hands of those who think the colour description of the jelly bean/gum drop they chose is valid for them as they perceive themselves

4. (About ¾ of the participants should raise their hands.)

5. Emphasize the following: No one is just "one colour", but one colour is usually dominant. All of us have some of the various traits associated with other colours.

WALK APART-OR WALK TOGETHER

Aim	Understanding individual differences and similarities
Group Size	10-12 Participants
Materials	Flipchart, Marker, enough space for participants to form a line side by side.
Duration	90 minutes

Description

1. Two "volunteers" come forward and stand with backs together. The "audience" is asked to call out things about these two volunteers that are different. Differences sometimes push us apart. As each difference is called the volunteers take one step apart.

2. When the reach the end of available space, have them turn and face each other. Now the audience is asked to call out things that are similar/alike about the volunteers. As each similarity is called out, the volunteers take one step toward each other.

3. Note, most times the differences are things we can see: hair/skin colour, wearing glasses or not, different type shoe, one in pants, the other in skirt.

4. The similarities are often times things that the audience perceives: both are ???, both are enthusiastic, etc. Of course there may be some physical characteristics that are similar.

5. Facilitate a discussion on what happened to empathise with the person on their role card and guess which rights are important to them.

SECTION SEVEN:

STEREOTYPE THINKING

`JUST WHAT DO YOU SEE?

Aim	To encourage the participants to realize that each team member/co-worker "sees a different picture," that each viewpoint is valid, and that understanding what the other person sees benefits the workplace.
Participants	Any size group of more than five participants
Materials	Handout (Picture of a flower)

Duration   10-15 Minutes

Instructions:

1. Tell the participants that as an introduction to the day (morning/ afternoon/topic), you want to have some fun. Pass out the hand out.

2. Tell the participants that they have 60 seconds to look at the picture and then identify the colours in the picture.

3. Time them and when one minute is up, call out, "Time's up!"

4. Ask them: "How many people identified three colours?"

5. "How many people identified four colours?"

6. "Five colours?

7. "More than five colours?"

8. Ask participants to tell you the names of the colours they saw (start with those participants who identified LESS colours).

9. Write the names of the colours down on a flipchart or whiteboard. (Most people will respond with the following colours: pink, green, orange, yellow and purple.

10. Other people will add colours such as raspberry, mustard, gold, magenta, salmon, indigo, jade (yes, there's a tiny bit of jade in the lower left corner), and mauve.)

11. If the participants do not identify colours other than pink, green, orange, yellow and purple, tell them that the colours you see in the picture also include raspberry, mustard, gold, magenta, salmon, indigo, jade, and mauve.

12. As an interesting aside, you might want to ask those participants who identified more colours if they had any specific training (art school, graphic design courses, fashion design training, etc.) which helped develop this colour sense. This could be further developed in the debriefing.

13. Just as the different participants saw different colours in the picture, so life has painted with different colours a picture into our lives. Few of us have had the same life experiences as the person sitting next to us, or the person working with us.

Team Building

14. Because each person sees things differently, conflict can arise. This conflict can negatively impact our work. However, we can turn this

potential negative to a positive by learning how to see with the other person's eyes and see what they are "seeing."

15. Doing this results in greater creativity and better problem-solving. We all bring different skills, abilities and life experiences to the team. We need to appreciate and use each member's talents in order to obtain the BEST results.

Motivation

1. Because of these different experiences and viewpoints, we react differently to different stimuli - what motivates one person does not motivate another. Some people might be highly motivated by money. Others could care less about money as long as they have funds enough to pay the bills.

2. But feeling they are respected by their boss and their ideas are listened to might motivate them. Successful motivators understand how the other person "sees" and use this knowledge to provide behaviours/rewards that motivate that individual.

Communication

1. Because each person sees things differently, misunderstandings can arise. These misunderstandings can have negative consequences in the workplace and can develop into conflict.

2. Good communication skills involve understanding the other person's point of view. This involves listening to understand, not half-hearted listening or listening to gain ammunition against a particular viewpoint.

Problem-Solving

3. Because each person sees things differently, conflict can arise. This conflict can negatively impact our work and our relationships with co-workers (it is human nature to view people who are different as being inferior to ourselves).

4. However, we can turn this potential negative to a positive by learning how to see with the other person's eyes and see what they are "seeing." Doing this results in greater creativity and better problem-solving.

Conflict Management

1. What one person sees as positive flexibility, another perceives as negative disorder.

2. What one person views as driving towards a goal, another sees as stifling creativity.

3. Because each person sees things differently, conflict can arise. This conflict can negatively impact our work. However, we can turn this potential negative to a positive by learning how to see with the other person's eyes and listen to what they are "seeing." Doing this results in greater creativity and better problem-solving.

4. NOTE: See if any person noted more than six colours. There were only six lines for colour names and most people will stop at six. That doesn't make for exemplary problem-solving.

5. **Variation**: Instead of asking participants what colours they see in an image, ask them to remember back to their childhood when they used to stare up at the clouds and see ever changing pictures in them.

6. Project a cloud photo onto a screen and ask them to write down the various shapes they see in the clouds.

PICTURES ARE WORTH
A THOUSAND WORDS

Aim	To understand how society makes assumptions about people based on their background and/or socioeconomic status. (This exercise can be used as a lead-in to discussions of stereotyping as well.)
Group Size	10-40

Materials Copies of "Pictures Are Worth a Thousand Words" handouts (Parts One and Two), file folders, pictures of personalities used in the exercise, biographical information on these personalities, and writing utensils

Duration 1 hour of preparation, two class periods for the exercise itself.

Instructions

1. Preparation work is required for this activity. First, pick 12–15 well known people who have backgrounds that are unusual or unexpected (e.g., Hitler wanted to be an artist, etc.). Create a brief biographical profile on each.

2. A profile of 12 such personalities is provided. Feel free to create your own profiles modeled after these examples.

3. Create a folder for each personality. On the exterior of the file folder, secure a picture of a personality, print that person's name, and include an alphabetic identifier (e.g., Folder A, Folder B, etc.). The pictures chosen should be big enough to see from a distance. On the inside of the folder, secure a biography (see examples provided) or an article about the personality.

4. **Day 1:** Distribute Part One of the "Pictures Are Worth a Thousand Words" handout.

5. Give participants 10 - 15 minutes to read over the profiles and answer the questions on the hand out. Next, transition into

Part Two with these questions:

1. Do you think you know who any of these people are? Which ones?
2. Who do you think they are?
3. Are there any specific profiles that you think sound particularly interesting? Why?
4. Who on this list do you think is the most successful?

5. Next, distribute Part Two of the "Pictures Are Worth a Thousand Words" hand-out. Display the file folders with the images of the personalities at the front of the classroom.

6. Give the participants 10– 15 minutes to match the personalities to the faces/names using the letters printed on the folders (e.g., A = Malcolm X). Announce the correct answers and discuss the matches that were incorrect. Finally, split the participants into groups of three or four people.

7. Each group should be assigned one of the personalities used in the exercise.

8. Their assignment for the following day will be to read the biographical information provided on that particular personality.

Day 2: Give participants 10 – 15 minutes to get into their groups and create a two- to three-minute presentation to the class. Their presentation should address the following issues:

- What were some assumptions you made about this person before you knew who they were?
- Why did you make these assumptions?
- Were these assumptions proven to be correct or incorrect?
- Questions that every group should answer are:
- Are assumptions like these positive or negative? Why and in what way?
- How do they affect the way that we treat others?

- What has this exercise taught you about making assumptions?

Example Personality Profiles

Personality A: Malcolm X
- Was sent to live in various foster homes and orphanages after his mother was admitted into a mental hospital
- Wanted to be a lawyer, but was told by a teacher that those dreams were "unrealistic"
- Became involved in various narcotic, prostitution and gambling rings after moving to
- New York
  For more information:
  http://www.cmgww.com/historic/malcolm/about/bio.htm

Personality B: Jerry Springer
- Child of Jewish refuges of the Holocaust
- Worked on Robert Kennedy's presidential campaign
- Was mayor of a U.S. city
- For more information:
  http://www.answers.com/topic/jerry-springer

Personality C: Adolf Hitler
- Was a good student for quite some time but grades began to slip in high school
- Had dreams of becoming an artist and, at age of 18, moved away from home to be closer to a major art school

- Worked odd jobs and was even homeless while trying to get into art school
  For more information:
  http://www.netcomuk.co.uk/~lenin/ADOLF_HITLER_BIOGRAP.html#biog

Personality D: M.C. Hammer

- Born into a very religious family
- Worked for the Oakland Athletics baseball team
- Wanted to play baseball for a living, but joined the Navy instead

For more information:
http://music.uk.launch.yahoo.com/ar-301341-bio—MC-Hammer

Personality E: Al Capone

- Quit school in the 6th grade
- Worked in a bowling alley and a candy shop
- Is from a very close-knit family

For more information:
http://flfl.essortment.com/alcapone_rtub.htm

Personality F: Oprah Winfrey

- Grew up very poor and lived with grandmother on a farm in Mississippi
- Later lived with mother, but was rebellious and got into a lot of trouble
- Was a parent at the age of 14
- For more information:
  http://ks.essortment.com/oprahwinfrey_rkcr.htm

Personality G: Bill Gates

- Dropped out of Harvard

- Refused to do school work in Jr. High and High School
- Involved with building projects through Habitat for Humanity

For more information:
http://inventors.about.com/library/inventors/blbillgates.htm?once=true&

Personality H: Maya Angelou

- After experiencing a traumatic event, completely stopped talking for almost four years
- Dropped out of high school
- Best friend was a brother named Bailey

For more information:
http://project1.caryacademy.org/echoes/poet_Maya_Angelou/Angelou'sBiography.htm

Personality I: Drew Barrymore

- Born into a family or actors
- Was a child star
- Abused drugs and alcohol beginning at a young age

For more information:
http://allstars-online.net/Drewbio.html

Personality J: Cuba Gooding, Jr.

- As a child, family lived in a car after being evicted from their home
- Started a dance group called Majestic Vision Dance breakers
- Performed at the 1984 Olympic Games

For more information:
http://www.biggeststars.com/c/cuba_gooding_jr._biography.html

Personality K: Osama Bin Laden

- Born 17th child out of 52 children
- Family owned a construction company
- Family was very wealthy; father was a billionaire

For more information:

http://www.infoplease.com/spot/osamabinladen.html

Personality L: Tupac Shakur

Was named after an Incan Indian who was a revolutionary

Loved to write poetry and love songs

Attended The Baltimore School for the Performing Arts; studied acting and ballet

For more information:

PICTURES ARE WORTH A THOUSAND WORDS

Part One Handout

Directions: Read the following profiles of well-known people. After reading each profile, list words that come to your mind based on the background information provided about the person.

Think about things like what that person may do for a living, their race, their gender, and the things that may be important to them. Make note of what you think this person may be well known for. Guess the individual's name and record it in the blank provided.

Personality A:

• Was sent to live in various foster homes and orphanages after mother was admitted into a mental hospital

• Wanted to be a lawyer, but was told by a teacher that those dreams were "unrealistic"

• Became involved in various narcotic, prostitution and gambling rings after moving to New York

Notes:

Who am I? _____

Personality B:

• Child of Jewish refuges of the Holocaust

• Worked on Robert Kennedy's presidential campaign

• Was mayor of a U.S. city

Notes:

Who am I? _____

Personality C:

• Was a good student for quite some time but grades began to slip in high school

• Had dreams of becoming an artist, and at age of 18, moved away from home to be closer to a major art school

• Worked odd jobs and was even homeless while trying to get into art school

Notes:

Who am I? _____

Personality D:

• Born into a very religious family

• Worked for the Oakland Athletics baseball team

• Wanted to play baseball for a living, but joined the Navy instead

Notes:

Who am I? _____

Personality E:

• Quit school in the 6th grade

• Worked in a bowling alley and a candy shop

• Is from a very close-knit family

Notes:

Who am I? _____

Personality F:

• Grew up very poor and lived with grandmother on a farm in Mississippi

• Later lived with mother, but was rebellious and got into a lot of trouble

• Was a parent at the age of 14

Notes:

Who am I? _____

Personality G:

• Dropped out of Harvard

• Refused to do school work in Jr. High and High School

• Involved with building projects through Habitat for Humanity

Notes:

Who am I? _____

Personality H:

• Experienced a traumatic event and completely stopped talking for almost four years

• Dropped out of high school

• Best friend was a brother named Bailey

Notes:

Who am I? _____

Personality I:

• Born into a family of actors

• Was a child star

• Abused drugs and alcohol beginning at a young age

Notes:

Who am I? _____

Personality J:

• As a child, family lived in a car after being evicted from their home

• Started a dance group called Majestic Vision Dance breakers

• Performed at the 1984 Olympic Games

Notes:

Who am I? _____

Personality K:

• Born 17th child out of 52 children

• Family owned a construction company

• Family was very wealthy; father was a billionaire

Notes:

Who am I? _____

Personality L:

• Was named after an Incan Indian who was a revolutionary

• Loved to write poetry and love songs

• Attended the Baltimore School for the Performing Arts; studied acting and ballet

Notes:

Who am I? _____

THE STEREOTYPE WATCH

Aim   1. To introduce the concept of stereotype awareness as an (over)simplifying cognitive scheme.

2. To identify how it functions and how it is shared and perpetuated through socialisation

Group Size   10-30

Materials   The story of the big bad wolf!!

Duration   30 minutes

1. Room setting: Arrange room with chairs in circle (If the group is too numerous, divide participants into two groups). Use paper and scotch tape to design a watch inside the circle, in front of the chairs.

2. The theme of the watch aims at enhancing the dynamics of this exercise, to contribute at impregnating a rapid pace, as the results of the exercise depend on that.

3. Prepare sheets of A4 paper as many as the number of participants containing as headlines different categories (i.e. artist, Muslim, politician, Roma/Gypsy, Japanese, priest) or suggestive images.

4. Ask participants to sit on chairs.

5. Distribute the sheets of paper and explain that participants will have to associate the word/the image they see in headline with an adjective that comes first to their mind.

6. They will have to write the adjective on the paper and then pass the paper to the neighbour.

7. Explain rules of writing: from bottom to top and fold the paper over the adjective you wrote before handing the sheet of paper to the neighbour at left.

8. The trainer stands in the middle and dictates the shift of paper (tic-tac-tic).

9. Stop the exercise when papers have made one round.

10. Collect them and read them out briefly.

11. Pick some categories and write them on flipchart (if two groups, when reading out, write down the identical categories you gave to the groups).

12. **Debriefing ideas**

1. Degree of accuracy of the image (stereotype)

2. The simplification by categorisation

3. Are stereotypes bad?

4. Can stereotypes be avoided?

5. Are stereotypes shared image at society level?

6. How stereotypes are learnt in the process of socialisation?

7. How are stereotypes perpetuated/transmitted?

Optional Version

Purpose: Enable to acknowledge their own stereotypes.

Group: 20

Time: 10 minutes

Equipment: newspapers, music videos

Materials: none

Procedure

1. First, explain to the participants that the purpose of the exercise is to explore the myths and stereotypes that we learn and develop about others.

2. Explain that stereotypes almost always result from socialization from others and that even when we have a positive or negative experience interpreting that and drawing conclusions about the association between that experience and the social group is primarily the result of our socialization experiences and what we have been told or heard.

3. Then, explain to the participants that they should take the list of groups that you provide and mark them according to the following criteria:

4. Cross off the group to which you (each individual does this step alone) belong. Then, place an "X" beside any of the groups from whom you don't have a friend or acquaintance that belongs.

5. Then, beside each group, place a percentage beside the group that you think describes how closely that group is to the group to which you belong.

6. In other words, how alike are group A and group B? Then, once the participants have completed this step, either assign or allow them to divide themselves into heterogeneous groups so that they can discuss their answers.

7. Tell them to discuss with their group the reasons why they came to the conclusions they did. Tell them it is important for members of each group to discuss the answers.

Group Suggestions

This exercise can be done with any type of categorization that has at least three categories (religion, ethnicity, etc.)

THE STEREOTYPES

Stereotypes: The acknowledgment of our own stereotypes makes us more critical of our actions by allowing us to reflect on we treat others. This exercise will encourage participants to consider how their own preconceived judgments may shape their actions.

The aim of this activity is to enable participants to acknowledge their own stereotypes of people based on

1.   Race
2.   Gender
3.   Religion
4.   Sexuality
5.   Religion

Accent and other diversity and equality strands with a view to discussing their thought feelings and emotions regarding their perceptions of stereotypes these with others.

THE STEREOTYPE WATCH

This exercises introduces the concept of stereotype awareness about stereotypes as being and simplified cognitive scheme. Furthermore, this exercise aims to identify how stereotypes function in society and how they are perpetuated through socialisation.

This exercise introduces the concept of stereotype awareness about stereotypes as being and simplified cognitive scheme. Furthermore, this exercise aims to identify how stereotypes function in society and how they are perpetuated through socialisation.

It is said that our brains are simply **wired to stereotype** others, and we categorize people every day by race, gender, religion, ethnic background. However, it is when people use these stereotypes for things like discrimination or even hate crimes that one can really see the true dangers of stereotyping.

The **negative effects of stereotyping** are the use of laws and rules created where some people benefit and others do not. For example, the Jim Crow laws of the south would be an example of the consequences of negative stereotyping, which suggests that black people are inferior.

Even **positive stereotyping** can be harmful to groups and individuals. For example, Asian Americans are seen as the model minority community. This should be positive, but it puts undue pressure on these individuals to succeed. This can lead to effects like higher suicide rates.

This is especially hard on Asians refugees such as the Hmong in the USA and the Bangladeshi community in the UK. They are supposed to be exceptionally smart and driven, according to the stereotypes about Asians, so they do not have the skills to meet the stereotypes. Society, therefore, sees them as burdens because they do not fit the views that people have.

In an era in which the ideal body image is marketed in the media, the **psychological internalisation of stereotyping** which suggest that women are supposed to be very thin can be very harmful to a woman's self-esteem.

This **internalization** can lead to self-destructive behaviours, such as eating disorders, and spending that would help them perpetuate this image, such as fashion, plastic surgery, makeup, or exercise equipment.

Political stereotyping: In recent times, the effect of stereotyping is such that it stops us from learning about these groups. For example, if a person believes all Muslims are terrorists, that person that person may be unwilling to learn about Islam, the same principle also applied to those who have taken on board stereotypes which suggest that all Arabs are potential terrorists, especially after the tragic events of 9/11 in the UK and 7/7 in the UK.

A-B-C-DIVERSITY

Aim	To understand the implications of Ageism
Group Size	Any size
Materials	Newsprint and markers or flip chart one index card for each participant; container (such as a paper sack, shoebox, or hat); pens/pencils
Duration	30-40 minutes

Instruction:

1. Consider the fact that most, if not all people have participated in prejudice and/or discrimination. Most of us have disliked some group because of qualities or characteristics we believed it possessed.

2. Some of us have treated people unfairly because of prejudices we hold. At the very least, we have told, laughed at or listened to a joke that made fun of one group or another.

3. Because racism is a volatile topic, group leaders may focus on one of the other "isms," such as sexism, ageism or heterosexism.

4. If issues regarding racism do not surface, do not feel like you must bring them up. Be open to teens' experiences and perceptions and allow the discussion to go in the direction it needs.

5. If teens want to discuss experiences of racism, be prepared to help them articulate their feelings in a constructive way.

6. On two pieces of newsprint or the board, prepare a very large illustration, like the one below. You will need room inside the boxes to write responses:

    a)   Names I've been called

    b)   Names I've called others

    c)   Time when I was treated unfairly

    d)   Time when I was unfair to others

For Step 10, create a poster of the A B C's of diversity as outlined below:

A - Attitude (prejudice)

B - Behaviour (discrimination)

C - Consequences (physical, emotional or economic injury)

Procedure:

1. Remind teens that stereotyped thinking forces group members into a mould and ignore the fact that everyone is first an individual and second a member of a group. Explain that this activity will demonstrate the harm of stereotypes.

2. Distribute index cards and display the illustration you have drawn. Have teens draw horizontal and vertical lines on their index cards so they look like your illustration.

3. Review the four boxes on the illustration and explain that you will collect the cards and read responses anonymously, so no one will see what anyone wrote. Emphasize that honesty is important.

After each instruction, allow time for teens to write responses:

1. In the **upper left hand box**, write names you have been called because of your age, racial or ethnic background, physical characteristics, religion, presumed sexual orientation or any other characteristic

2. In the **upper right hand box**, write names you have called other people for similar reasons.

3. In the **lower left hand box**, describe a time when you were treated unfairly because of a particular characteristic such as race, religion, age and so on.

4. In the **lower right hand box**, describe a time when you treated someone unfairly for a similar reason.

5. Allow time for everyone to finish, then collect the cards and put them in your container.

6. Draw cards at random and read aloud the responses. Write responses on the large illustration. If you run out of room, read quickly through the remaining cards so everyone can hear the names people in the group have been called.

7. Do not comment on the names at this point.

8. Repeat the process for boxes 2, 3 and 4, without comment. Abbreviate the "unfair treatments" in boxes 3 and 4 by just writing the behaviours (for example, spit on, laugh at, tease, and beat up) on the board.

9. Ask the group to look at the large list of names and examples of unfair treatment.

10. Ask for volunteers who have been called names or treated unfairly to talk about their experiences.

11. Help them to focus on the feelings they had when being discriminated against. Then encourage others to talk about name calling or unfair treatment they have been responsible for.

12. Write the term "prejudice" on newsprint or the board and ask for a definition. Work toward a definition consistent with the following:

13. Prejudice: a certain attitude, usually negative, toward a particular group or member of that group. Prejudice is usually toward strangers, who may have a certain appearance. The word comes from Latin words meaning Prejudge.

14. Prejudice happens whenever we prejudge others because of race, religion, age, gender, physical size or appearance, occupation, social class, sexual orientation and so on.

15. We decide how we feel about them before we know them.

16. Write the term "discrimination" on newsprint or the board and ask for a definition like the following:

17. Discrimination: different, usually unfair, treatment of a group or member of that group, because of prejudiced feelings about them. The word comes from the Latin word for "divide."

18. Discrimination happens whenever we divide or separate people into groups (physically or in our minds) and treat one group unfairly or unequally because of our prejudices about their race, religion, age, gender, physical size or appearance, occupation, social class, sexual orientation and so on.

19. Display the A-B-Cs of diversity poster. Clarify what each letter represents.

20. Ask the group for examples of prejudiced attitudes, unfair behaviours and negative consequences they have observed or experienced.

21. Emphasize that there are always consequences when a person is treated with prejudice or discrimination.

22. The consequences can be emotional, such as hurt feelings or anger, or they can be physical, such as giving up on a job or punching someone.

Conclude the activity using the Discussion Points.

1. How does it feel to talk about prejudice and discrimination?

2. Look back at the names people said they have been called.

3. How might they have felt when called those names?

4. What about people who name call or treat others unfairly?

5. Do the people who feel prejudice and discriminate against others experience any consequences? If so, what? (Answer: Today there are laws against discrimination and anyone accused of discriminating against others in the workplace can be prosecuted. There are, however, no laws against feeling prejudice.)

6. What is the difference between prejudice and discrimination? (Answer: Prejudice is having an attitude about someone; discrimination is behaving a certain way toward someone.)

7. You can look at what we have written and tell if people in this group have suffered from prejudice and discrimination.

8. What could you do to make up for some of that? (Answers may include: Apologize to each other; don't let it happen again; get to know one another better; don't tolerate prejudice or discrimination when it happens.)

A-B-C-DIVERSITY

Notes: A stereotype is generally defined as a generalization about a group of people where people use a very simple pattern for judging an entire group of people. Stereotypes are mental shortcuts that enable individuals to reduce the amount of cognitive effort they spend on categorizing others into groups and, instead, focus attention on important events or people.

7. **Realistic conflict theory** can be used to understand why unpleasant stereotypes regarding low socioeconomic individuals have formed.

8. This theory would assert that individuals in higher classes might feel the need to protect the resources they have and, therefore, may develop hostility towards others trying to advance, such as those in a lower economic class.

9. The **concept of stereotype threat** states that a person will attempt to act opposite a stereotype if they feel that another person will judge them accordingly.

10. **The negative socioeconomic stereotype** is an external locus of control of reinforcement which says that a reward or punishment will

reinforce behaviour if a person perceives the reward or punishment as dependent on his or her behaviour.

11. In other words, one holds a view of **internal control of reinforcement** if the person believes that what happens to him or her is a result of his or her behaviour, whereas an **external locus of control** is when one believes his or her behaviour does not affect the reward or punishment.

12. Low socioeconomic status can lead to higher external control of Stereotypes about individuals of low socioeconomic status is particularly difficult to overcome. The stereotype, whether it stems from a mental shortcut or from competition over scarce resources, causes a **self-fulfilling prophecy** where an individual acts according to the stereotype. **Stereotype threat causes** the individual to be very aware of the stereotype and by attempting to act opposite the stereotype, actually validates the stereotype.

MAKE A DIFFERENCE

Aim

To examine the behaviours that lead to becoming an open-minded and non-judgmental contributing member of a diverse team

Material: Covered flipchart prepared in advance (see Trainer's Notes)

Procedure

1. Explain that this activity offers team members the opportunity to examine their own perspectives in relation to diversity issues.

2. Pair up the participants and uncover the flipchart.

3. Tell the participants to examine the "Diverse Team Actions That Make a Difference" on the flipchart and ask the pairs to discuss how those actions can affect team performance.

4. Instruct the pairs to come up with additional "actions" and write them down. Allow 5-10 minutes.

5. Have the pairs call out their suggested "actions" and add them to the list on the flipchart.

6. Reconvene the full group and discuss the additions to the list and how they will affect a diverse team. Summarize by asking questions like:

   a.   Are these "actions" easy or difficult?

   b.   Are they actually realistic?

   c.   How do you rank yourselves on these points?

   d.   If personal changes become necessary, is it worth it?

Debrief

As a member of a team, each person has a special responsibility, and sometimes it takes extra effort to be a valuable team member where diversity issues are involved. There are no firm answers, but there is strong evidence that those people who are working toward being open-minded and non-judgmental are considered extremely valuable to a diverse team.

Trainer Notes:

Ahead of time, prepare the flipchart as shown below:

Diverse Team Actions That Make a Difference

1. Looking beyond first impressions to judge a fellow team member.
2. Trying to pronounce a difficult name of a team member who prefers to be called by his or her correct name.
3. Understanding that diverse employees have different perspectives that can contribute greatly to the team.
4. Being willing to openly discuss diversity issues.

MAKE A DIFFERENCE

Make A Difference: To examine the behaviours that lead to becoming an open-minded and non-judgmental contributing member of a diverse team.

The purpose of this exercise is to enable participants to have a greater understanding of judgemental views when working in team that is diverse by way, of race, gender, sexuality, religion etc, thus enabling participants to have a deeper understanding how and why the concepts of being open and being none judgemental should be viewed through the lens by way of the following in order that team conflicts can be resolved, strategies for reaching an agreement:

- Survival Mechanism,
- Personal Choice,
- Extreme Judgement,
- Conditioning,
- Resolving Team Conflict
- Understanding the Situation
- How to Reach an Agreement

Survival Mechanism

At the most basic level, judgement is nothing more than a survival mechanism. The ego mind labels things based on their perceived impact on one's survival. So when one feels that they are under threat in some way, a judgement will be made.

Personal Choice

What people do or do not do is then up to them, as long as it does not hurt another person. Just because one feels a strong reaction to what another person does, it doesn't mean that it is wrong or bad. It could simply be the way that they are expressing themselves and how they choose to live their life.

Extreme Judgement

So if one is extremely judgemental to others or towards certain things and their own survival is not at risk, then it could seem strange and even confusing. How one interprets the world and what they see as right or wrong, is a result of what is going on within them.

Conditioning

These feelings, emotions, wants and needs are not right or wrong, they are simply part of the human experience. But due to things such as ones upbringing, education, religion and social conditioning, the mind is taught to accept some things and reject others. Instinctive If human beings couldn't make judgments they would last for very long on this planet. To be overly judgemental can be a sign that one needs to let go off the conflict that has built up within.

Resolving Team Conflict:

Conflict is pretty much inevitable when you work with others. People have different viewpoints and under the right set of circumstances, those differences escalate to conflict. How you handle that conflict determines whether it works to the team's advantage, or contributes to its demise. When a team oversteps the mark of healthy difference of opinion, resolving conflict requires respect and patience.

The Three-Stage Process below is a form of mediation process, which helps team members to do this:

Step 1: Prepare for Resolution

Acknowledge the conflict – The diversity related conflict has to be acknowledged before it can be managed and resolved. The tendency is for people to ignore the first signs of any issue relating to diversity related conflict.

Discuss the impact – As a team, discuss the impact of the diversity and equality issue is having on team dynamics and performance.

Agree to a cooperative process – Everyone involved must agree to cooperate in to resolve the conflict. This means putting the team first, and may involve setting aside your opinion or ideas for the time being.

Agree to communicate – The most important thing throughout the resolution process is for everyone to keep communications open. The people involved need to talk about the issue and discuss their strong feelings.

Active listening is essential here because to move on you need to really understand where the other person is coming from.

Step 2: Understand the Situation

Once the team is ready to resolve the conflict, the next stage is to understand the situation, and each team member's point of view. Take time to make sure that each person's position is heard and understood.

Clarify positions – Whatever the conflict or disagreement, it's important to clarify people's positions. Whether there are obvious factions within the team who support a particular option, approach or idea, each position needs to be clearly identified and articulated by those involved.

Analyze in smaller groups – Break the team into smaller groups, separating people who are in alliance. In these smaller groups, analyze and dissect each position, and the associated facts, assumptions and beliefs.

Convene back as a team – After the group dialogue, each side is likely to be much closer to reaching agreement. The process of uncovering facts and assumptions allows people to step away from their emotional attachments and see the issue more objectively.

Step 3: How to Reach an Agreement

Now that all parties understand the others' positions, the team must decide what decision or course of action to take. With the facts and assumptions considered, it's easier to see the best of action and reach agreement.

Stop and cool off – There is little point in trying to talk through the issues when both people are upset. Give it a little time and let tempers cool down. Come together when each party has achieved some sort of equilibrium.

Have everyone talk and listen to each other – Make sure that nobody is hiding from the issue at hand. Keep everyone talking and expressing themselves honestly and openly.

Find out what everyone needs – Sometimes these dialogues can focus on complaints rather than developing solutions. Determine what everyone needs from the situation and strive for a solution where everyone's needs are met.

Brainstorm solutions – Everyone will have their own vision of an ideal outcome for themselves. The challenge will be to avoid forcing our solutions on the conflict situation and allow solutions to emerge out of creative thinking on everyone's part.

Choose the idea that everyone can live with – One of the ways to break from a negative conflict cycle is to find solutions that you all feel are fair under the circumstances.

Create a plan and implement it – To make sure that the conflict does not re-emerge, you must make a blueprint. Plan ways of working together that will keep emotional outbursts to a minimum.

THE SURGEON'S DILEMMA

Aim   To understand the consequences of
                    generalized thinking in relation to
                    stereotypes

Group Size   15 – 35

Materials   Scenario: Surgeon's Dilemma

Duration   15 - 30 minutes

Procedure:

Surgeon's Dilemma

A young man who had been badly injured in a car accident has been brought into a hospital's accident and emergency department. The doctor determines that emergency brain surgery is required. Accordingly, the brain surgeon is paged. Upon seeing the patient, the surgeon exclaims, 'My God, I can't operate on that boy! He's my son!'

That is so, but the surgeon is not the boy's father. How can the apparent contradiction be explained

Solution

The answer, of course, is that the surgeon is the boy's mother. Although there are many women doctors - and many of them prominent specialists - our cultural stereotyping tells us that doctors are men and nurses are women.

Red or Black

1. This is a good exercise to use in a negotiating course. It demonstrates how people work with each other and shows how trust can be built or destroyed.

2. Divide the group into pairs and give each pair a pack of cards with the jokers removed.

3. Inform everyone that the objective of this card game is to end up with a positive accumulative score after playing seven rounds.

4. The person with the higher positive score will win a prize.

5. Zero is not a positive score. The facilitator gets the prize if neither person gets a positive score or if the final score is tied.

6. Each round consists of both people selecting a red or black card and putting it face down on the table. Both cards are turned over and scores are awarded as follows:

You Select	Partner Selects	Your Score	Partner's Score
RED	RED	-1	-1
RED	BLACK	+2	-2
BLACK	RED	-2	+2
BLACK	BLACK	+1	+1

There are seven rounds and the last two rounds score double. If both players agree, they can talk to each other after round two and then again after round five. They should remain silent for the rest of the game

SECTION EIGHT:

CULTURAL DIVERSITY

SOLO

Aim	Enable participants to identify and reflect on the elements that build their own identity.
Group Size	Any size; from 15 year old onwards
Material	Preferably an outdoor place in nature (e.g. beach or forest).
Duration	40 minutes (including 10 minutes for self-reflection).

PROCEDURE

1. Inform participants that assessing their own selves will be the starting point to reflect about inclusion and diversity, and that they will have 10 minutes of "solo time" for self-reflection.

2. Take the group of participants outdoors (the beach or the forest is a convenient setting) and gather participants at a designated "meeting point".

3. Introduce the activity: "There are many aspects to identity, some hidden some visible. Take 10 minutes individually to reflect on how you perceive yourself: what makes you the person you are today?"

4. Having the "meeting point" as the reference point, instruct participants to select a private place that allows them sufficient distance from each other and at the same time keeps them in view of one another; instruct participants, when they are standing in their private place, they should draw a circle around themselves (in the ground) and stay 10 minutes inside the circle, in silence, using the time and the "stillness" for self-reflection; instruct participants to come back to the "meeting point" as soon as you - as the facilitator- give a signal (e.g. wave your arms or whistle).

5. After 10 minutes, give the signal so participants can step out of the circle and gather at the "meeting point".

6. Building the symbolic private space around each person is important for the success of the activity. If you are standing in soft soil like at the

beach just use your finger to draw a circle around you; if you are standing in a hard soil like the forest, make use of the nature around you to mark your circle – like pebbles, leaves and small branches.

7. Whatever method you use, put forward a few questions to facilitate self-reflection, such as:

- Which elements build you as a person?

- How would you describe yourself?

- Which experiences of inclusion and which experiences of diversity were significant in building the person you are today?

- At what times do you usually feel included and/or excluded?

- How do you feel now, at this precise moment?

- What is making you feel comfortable?

- What is making you feel uncomfortable?

8. If you are working with a particularly determined group of young people where you know there might be resistance, it is crucial to share the aims and possible benefit of such activity – and look for common agreement before exposing the young people to it.

9. The Solo activity can be used to demonstrate the value of turning self-reflection into a routine in order to conduct a coherent and accurate plan of action - both on a social and individual level.

10. Whatever methods you may apply, we believe it is crucial for you as a youth leader, as well as valuable for the young people, to allocate time for assessing your own feelings and evaluating your own actions on a continuous basis, in order to lucidly direct and re-direct change.

IS YOUR EVERYDAY LIFE REALLY DIVERSE?
INTERVIEW "OUTSIDE YOUR WALLS"

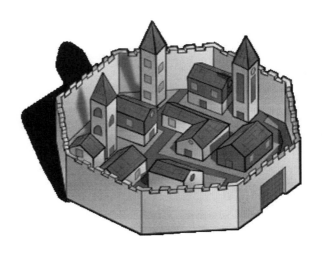

Aim	To encourage participants to interact with others outside of their culture or social group
Group	10-40
Material	"Interview Outside Your Walls" hand-out, writing utensils.

Duration   This is an out-of-class assignment. Participants
                      should be given at least two nights to complete
                      the assignment.

Instructions: Distribute the "Interview Outside Your Walls" hand-out.

1. Explain to participants that they are required to interview someone
   whose culture, race, age, religion, family background, etc. differs from
   their own.

2. The person they interview cannot be from the student's group of
   friends. Participants will record the interviewee's responses to the
   interview questions.

3. Participants will write about their experience afterward

INTERVIEW

"OUTSIDE YOUR WALLS"

Directions: To eliminate prejudice, we must know people not as a
colour or a type of clothing, but as individuals. Therefore, we have to
reach out beyond our walls to find new friends. Discovering that we
share things in common with people who are "different" from us helps
break down those walls. It brings us together as one race—the human
race.

Your task is to interview someone who is not of your culture, race, age, religion, family background, etc. In other words, you are to interview someone who is not in your current circle of friends. Use the following questions as your guide, but feel free to create your own questions too. When your interview is done, summarize your experiences on the back of this sheet. Talk especially about things that you had in common with the person. Also address whether you think it is important to have a diverse group of friends.

Name   of
Interviewee_____

Date of Interview: _____

Questions:

1. What is your favourite holiday? Why is it your favourite?

2. Do you listen to music? If so, who's your favourite group or artist?

3. Where is your favourite place to vacation? Why?

4. If you could only have one kind of food to eat for the rest of your life, what would it be?

5. Do you collect anything? Do you have any other hobbies?

6. Would you rather play or watch sports? Why?

7. Name your favourite movie, book, or television show.

8. Describe the weather on your "perfect day."

9. What is your favourite animal?

10. What is your idea of a "perfect day?

THE SALAD BOWL

Aim	To help participants understand each other.
Group	Any
Materials	A3 papers, pens, scotch/blue tack to stick papers on the wall,
Duration	Any.

Activity

1. Explain to the participants that you will be making (drawing) a salad.

2. On an easel pad, draw the bowl.

3. Ask the Group, "What would you like on your salad?" (Eg: lettuce, cucumbers, tomatoes, and croutons.)

4. Draw them on top of the salad bowl. If someone says "dressing", reply "We are not ready for the dressing, but will talk about it later."

5. Make the analogy that the bowl represents Girl Scouts and the salad ingredients are the variety of people in Girl Scouts.

6. Ask the Group to identify what some of the salad ingredients could symbolize. (eg: lettuce = different ages, cucumbers = beliefs, tomatoes = religions, olives = hair colour, croutons = ethnicity)

7. Then tell them that we are ready for the dressing.

8. Make the analogy that the dressing symbolizes pluralism. Refer to the chart with the definition of pluralism. "Dressing is Girl Scouting ... it gets on all of us, but it doesn't change us from being a tomato, or an olive ... but it's what enhances us all ... it binds us together ... it what makes us all part of this salad ... it makes us the Girl Scout salad.

MY NAME AND ITS ORIGIN

Aim	To understand each other and our respective communities.
Group	10-40
Material	The template, markers and free space in which the participants can speak in small groups.
Duration	20 Minutes

Description

1. Participants are requested to do an individual piece work. They should fill in the first 6 boxes of the grid within a few minutes (see download).

2. After the individual work, the participants are requested to create groups of five (5)

3. In the small groups the participants share and comment the form and the information about their names, trying to identify some common elements.

4. A small feedback to plenary with some funny findings can round off the exercise.

"MY NAME AND ITS ORIGIN" – TEMPLATE FOR GRID

My full name is	
But you can call me	
My name means	
It was given to me by	
Because	
Famous people with the same name as me	

NAME AND CULTURE

Mary Smith, an elderly Black woman, was in the recovery room after surgery. To assess her condition, the nurse, spoke her name, "Mary." The patient slowly opened her eyes and turned her head but made no further signs of acknowledgment. The nurse became concerned because most patients responded readily and clearly at this point. She called the woman Mrs. Smith. She then became alert, pleasant, and cooperative.

The Issue

1. The patient had perceived the use of her first name as a lack of respect and a form of racism. Nurses should refer to all adult patients as Mr., Miss, Ms., or Mrs., unless otherwise instructed.

2. To use a first name for anyone other than a close friend is both inappropriate and discourteous in most culture.

THE ORIGIN OF YOU NAME

Surnames didn't exist until approximately 1000 years ago. During the Middle Ages, but when family and town sizes began to grow, names became more descriptive, in order to be distinctive.

Actual surnames - names used throughout hereditary lineage - didn't come into use until about 1000 A.D in Europe. Members of royal families began the practice in many countries, choosing names according to their ancestral seats. But many of the **upper class** people didn't begin using surnames until the 14th century. The surnames that eventually developed drew their original meanings from **four** general categories:

Place Names: One common way to differentiate people was to describe them according to their geographic locations. If someone migrated from one spot to another, sometimes they were identified according to their original location. If a person lived near a river, forest, church, or other topographic feature, etc....

Patronymic Names: Last names created by a father's name were often used to create surnames, especially throughout Scandinavian countries. Such surnames were derived by adding a prefix meaning "son of" and "daughter of" the original name. Prefixes came from the language of the country, such as "Fitz" from the Norman languages; "Mac" from Gaelic languages' and "O" from Irish. Examples of patronymic names include Johnson (son of John), MacDonald (son of Donald), O'Brian (son of Brian), and Fitzhugh (son of Hugh).

Descriptive Names: Approximately 10% of all surnames were derived from physical characteristics of the first person to have that name. For example, if Michael had black hair, he became Michael Black. Peter the strong became Peter Strong.

Occupational Names: Occupational names were usually related to the specialty trades and crafts of the Middle Ages, and they are pretty self-explanatory. For example, a Miller worked grinding grain into flour; a Taylor made or repaired clothing;

Origin of Some African Names:

Ghana and the Ivory Coast frequently name their children after the day of the week they were born and the order in which they were born. Nigeria-Yorùbá names are traditionally classified into two categories:

Destiny Names (Situational) also known as Oruko Amutorunwa ("names assumed to be brought from heaven" or derived from a religious background)

Acquired Names ("given on earth" or granted by next of kin)

Although these basic surname classifications explain how many of today's surnames came into being, the variety of surnames continues to increase and expand. Therefore, if you want to research how your surname came to be, it is important to go through each generation and each family designation in order to arrive at the correct original name.

TIME CAPSULE

Aim

a) To get participants to think about who they are, things that are important to them, and things that have made them who they are. Also, to get participants thinking about how they want others to see them.

b) To get participants to share pieces of themselves, their values and their culture with other members of the group.

c) For other participants to show an interest in lives

of their group members and to be supportive of the sharing and self-disclosure that goes on.

Group   Any

Material   A box for each group
                     .

Duration   120 Minutes

Instructions:

1. Get boxes for each member of the group. If you choose, you can decorate the boxes in the group or outside of group time.

2. Tell the participants to pretend these boxes are time capsules that will be buried for 100 years. When they are dug up, people will know about them only from the items in the capsule and the way they are decorated.

3. Instruct the participants to fill the capsule with items that describe/show who they are, where they came from or how they feel. Items can include pictures, toys, etc. They can do this over the week then show and discuss with the group the items in each member's box and why they included them.

4. To get participants to think about who they are, things that are important to them, and things that have made them who they are. Also, to get participants thinking about how they want others to see them.

5. To get participants to share pieces of themselves, their values and their culture with other members of the group. For other participants to show an interest in lives of their group members and to be supportive of the sharing and self-disclosure that goes on.

Reflection:

a) The rationale behind this activity is that participants of other cultures spend a lot of time trying to fit in with the majority and often are not encouraged to share aspects of their culture that they are proud of.

b) This gives them the opportunity to be proud of themselves and their heritage. They are the experts on this subject and are being encouraged to share.

c) I think this will work because it is presented in a fun, futuristic, "let's pretend" manner, but they get to share items that represent themselves.

HELLO IN DIFFERENT LANGUAGES

Aim	To heighten cross-cultural awareness, celebrate cross-cultural knowledge, and to say "hello" in many different languages.
Group Size	1-5 or -1-10 Participants
Materials	Flipchart, Marker, Paper
Duration	15 minutes

Instructions:

1. Ask participants to see if they can guess how many people there are in the world and how many different languages are spoken. (There are 2800 languages and 6 billion people.)

2. If an equal number of people spoke each language, that would be 2 million people per language. You might relate this to local city/town size.).

3. Challenge the group to come up with as many different languages for "hello" as possible.

4. When somebody volunteers (e.g., Bonjour!), make sure they say it or repeat it clearly for the rest of the group who then repeat.

Optional:

1. Before people start making suggestions, ask the group to have a guess how many collective languages the group will be able to come up with.

2. Don't allow discussion - just do a quick whip around each person's guess and take a rough average - that's the group's estimate.

3. The group leader keeps count on his/her fingers. Was the final number of "hellos in different languages" close to the group's guess?

4. If the group underestimated, they may not realize the knowledge within the group that might be used to their advantage.

5. If the group's guess was an overestimate, why did they overestimate their knowledge resources?

Discussions:

Optional - to make more difficult or to add variation, try asking for these basic phrases:

Hello...Goodbye

Hello, My name is...?

Hello, How are you?

Yes...No

Please...Thank you

Do you speak English?

Optional, but recommended - have a list of hello in lots of different languages from which you can read out (see Jennifer's Language Page).

This is especially useful for groups, who don't know many different languages, as well as to learn, have fun, and illustrate the range of different languages. **Variation**: Can be run as a competition between groups.

CIRCLES

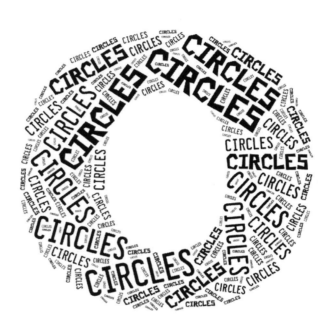

Aim

1. The purpose of this activity is to begin thinking about your level of interaction with people of different races and ethnicities.

2. Additionally, this activity will create a visual image of how often you interact with people of different races and ethnicities.

Group   10-15

Material   Flip Chart, Paper, Markers, Pens

Duration   20 Minutes

Procedures:

1. Write your name in the center circle and draw seven smaller circles connected to the larger **circle**.

2. In the smaller circles, write the names seven groups with which you identify

3. (Examples: gender, nationality/ethnicity, religious affiliation, political stance, geographic ties, family role, etc).

Debrief:

1. Ask individuals to get in small groups and answer the following questions:

2. Talk about a time when you felt proud to be a member of a certain group.

3. When did it feet painful to be a member of a certain group? What groups might be an asset or a challenge when you study abroad?

Different

Individuals

Valuing

Each other

Regardless of

Skin

Intellect

Talents or

Years

29277721R00160

Printed in Great Britain
by Amazon